Gr
Prefaces

_____

CORIOLANUS

Foreword by
Richard Eyre

NATIONAL

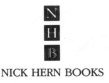

NICK HERN BOOKS

First published in this collected paperback edition in 1993 jointly by
Nick Hern Books Limited, 14 Larden Road, London W3 7ST
and the Royal National Theatre, London,
by arrangement with Batsford.

Preface to Coriolanus. Originally published in 1947

Set in 10/11 Baskerville by Pure Tech Corporation, Pondicherry
(India)
Printed in Australia by
Australian Print Group

A CIP catalogue record for this book is available from the British
Library

ISBN 1 85459 191 6

Shakespeare Alive!

The history of the theatre in England in this century can be told largely through the lives and work of two men: George Bernard Shaw and Harley Granville Barker, a triple-barrelled cadence of names that resonates like the ruffling of the pages of a large book in a silent public library. One was a brilliant polemicist who dealt with certainties and assertions and sometimes, but not often enough, breathed life into his sermons; the other a committed sceptic who started from the premise that the only thing certain about human behaviour was that nothing was certain. Both, however, possessed a passionate certainty about the importance of the theatre and the need to revise its form, its content, and the way that it was managed. Shaw was a playwright, critic and pamphleteer, Barker a playwright, director and actor.

The Voysey Inheritance is, at least in my opinion, Granville Barker's best play: a complex web of family relationships, a fervent but never unambiguous indictment of a world dominated by the mutually dependent obsessions of greed, class, and self-deception. It's also a virtuoso display of stagecraft: the writer showing that as director he can handle twelve speaking characters on stage at one time, and that as actor he can deal with the most ambitious and unexpected modulations of thought and feeling. The 'inheritance' of the Voyseys is a legacy of debt, bad faith, and bitter family dissension. Edward's father has, shortly before his death, revealed that he has been cheating the family firm of solicitors for many years, as his father had for many years before that. Towards the end of the play Edward Voysey, the youngest son, confronts the woman he loves:

EDWARD. Why wouldn't he own the truth to me about himself?

BEATRICE. Perhaps he took care not to know it. Would you have understood?

EDWARD. Perhaps not. But I loved him.

BEATRICE. That would silence a bench of judges.

Shaw would have used the story to moralise and polemicise. He might have had the son hate the father; he might have had him forgive him; he might have had him indict him as a paradigm of capitalism; he would never have said he loved him.

Everybody needs a father, or, failing that, a father-figure. He may be a teacher, a prophet, a boss, a priest perhaps, a political leader, a friend, or, sometimes, if you are very lucky, the real one. If you can't find a father you must invent him. In some ways, not altogether trivial, Granville Barker is something of a father-figure for me. He's a writer whom I admire more than any twentieth-century English writer before the sixties – Chekhov with an English accent; he's the first modern British director; he's the real founder of the National Theatre and, in his *Prefaces*, he's a man who, alone amongst Shakespearean commentators before Jan Kott, believed in the power of Shakespeare on stage.

There was a myth that Granville Barker was the natural son of Shaw. He was certainly someone whom Shaw could, in his awkward way, cherish and admire, educate and castigate. When Barker fell wildly in love ('in the Italian manner' as Shaw said) with Helen Huntington, an American millionairess, he married her, acquired a hyphen in his surname, moved first to Devon to play the part of a country squire, and then to France to a life of seclusion. Shaw thought that he had buried himself alive and could never reconcile himself to the loss. It was, as his biographer

Hesketh Pearson said: 'The only important matter about which he asked me to be reticent.'

After directing many of Shaw's plays for many years, acting many of his best roles (written by Shaw with Barker in mind), dreaming and planning together the birth of a National Theatre, not to mention writing, directing, and acting in his own plays while managing his own company at the Royal Court, Barker withdrew from the theatre, and for twenty years there was silence between the two men. Only on the occasion of the death of Shaw's wife did they communicate by letters. 'I did not know I could be so moved by anything,' wrote Shaw to him.

Out of this self-exile came one major work, slowly assembled over many years: *The Prefaces to Shakespeare*. With a few exceptions (Auden on *Othello*, Barbara Everett on *Hamlet*, Jan Kott on *The Tempest*) it's the only critical work about Shakespeare that's made any impact on me, apart, that is, from my father's view of Shakespeare, which was brief and brutal: 'It's absolute balls.'

As much as we need a good father, we need a good teacher. Mine, improbably perhaps, was Kingsley Amis. He'd arrived, somewhat diffidently, at Cambridge at the same time as I did. The depth of my ignorance of English literature corresponded almost exactly to his dislike of the theatre. Nevertheless, he made me see Shakespeare with a mind uncontaminated by the views of academics, whom he would never have described as his fellows and whose views he regarded as, well, academic. I would write essays marinated in the opinions of Spurgeon, Wilson Knight, Dover Wilson and a large cast of critical supernumeraries. He would gently, but courteously, cast aside my essay about, say, *Twelfth Night*: 'But what do *you* think of this play? Do you think it's any good?' 'Well ... er ... it's Shakespeare.' 'Yes, but is it any *good*? I mean as a *play*. It says it's a comedy. Fine. But does it have any decent jokes?'

I took this for irreverence, heresy even. Over the years, however, I've come to regard this as good teaching, or, closely allied, good direction. It's asking the right questions, unintimidated by reputation, by tradition, by received opinion, or by critical orthodoxy. This was shocking, but healthy, for a young and impressionable man ripe to become a fundamentalist in matters of literary taste and ready to revere F. R. Leavis as the Ayatollah of 'Cambridge English'. What you have is yourself and the text, only that. That's the lesson of Granville Barker: 'We have the text to guide us, half a dozen stage directions, and that is all. I abide by the text and the demands of the text and beyond that I claim freedom.' I can't imagine a more useful and more enduring dictum.

The Prefaces have a practical aim: 'I want to see Shakespeare made fully effective on the English stage. That is the best sort of help I can lend.' What Granville Barker wrote is a primer for directors and actors working on the plays of Shakespeare. There is lamentably little useful literature about the making of theatre, even though there is an indigestible glut of memoirs and biographies, largely concerned with events that have taken place *after* the curtain has fallen. If I was asked by a visiting Martian to recommend books which would help him, her or it to make theatre in the manner of the European I could only offer four books: Stanislavsky on *The Art of the Stage*, John Willett's *Brecht on Theatre*, Peter Brook's *The Empty Space*, and *The Prefaces to Shakespeare*.

Stanislavsky offers a pseudo-scientific dissection of the art of acting which is, in some respects, like reading Freud on the mechanism of the joke: earnest, well-meaning, but devoid of the indispensable ingredient of its subject matter: humour. Stanislavsky's great contribution was to demand that actors hold the mirror up to nature, that they take their craft as seriously as the writers they served, and to provide some sort of formal discipline within which both aims could be realised.

Brecht provided a manifesto that was a political and aesthetic response to the baroque encrustations of the scenery-laden, star-dominated, archaic boulevard theatre of Germany in the twenties. Although much of what he wrote as theory is an unpalatable mix of political ideology and artistic instruction, it is his theatrical instinct that prevails. He asserts, he insists, he browbeats. He demands that the stage, like society, must be re-examined, reformed, that the audience's habits mustn't be satisfied, they must be changed, but just when he is about to nail his 13 Articles to the church door he drops the voice of the zealot: 'The stage is not a hothouse or a zoological museum full of stuffed animals. It must be peopled with live, three-dimensional self-contradictory people with their passions, unconsidered utterances and actions.' In all art forms, he says, the guardians of orthodoxy will assert that there are eternal and immutable laws that you ignore at your peril, but in the theatre there is only one inflexible rule: 'The proof of the pudding is in the eating.' Brecht teaches us to ask the question: what goes on in a theatre?

Brook takes that question even further: what *is* theatre? It's a philosophical, but eminently practical, question that Brook has been asking for over 30 years and which has taken him to the African desert, a quarry in Iran, and an abandoned music hall in Paris. 'I take an empty space and call it a bare stage. A man walks across this empty space while someone else is watching him, and that is all that is needed for an act of theatre to be engaged.' For all his apparent concern with metaphyics, there is no more practical man of the theatre than Brook.

I was once at a seminar where someone asked him what was the job of the director. 'To get the actors on and off stage,' he said. Like Brecht, like Stanislavsky, like Granville Barker, Brook argues that for the theatre to be expressive it must be, above all, simple and unaffected: a distillation of language, of gesture, of action, of design, where meaning is the essence. The meaning must be felt as much as understood. 'They don't have to understand with their ears,' says Granville Barker, 'just with their guts.'

Brecht did not acknowledge a debt to Granville Barker. Perhaps he was not aware of one, but it seems to me that Barker's Shakespeare productions were the direct antecedents of Brecht's work. He certainly knew enough about English theatre to know that he was on to a good thing adapting *The Beggar's Opera*, *The Recruiting Officer* and *Coriolanus*. Brecht has been lauded for destroying illusionism; Granville Barker has been unhymned. He aimed at re-establishing the relationship between actor and audience that had existed in Shakespeare's theatre – and this at a time when the prevailing style of Shakespearean production involved *not* stopping short of having live sheep in *As You Like It*. He abolished footlights and the proscenium arch, building out an apron over the orchestra pit which Shaw said 'apparently trebled the spaciousness of the stage. . . . To the imagination it looks as if he had invented a new heaven and a new earth.'

His response to staging Shakespeare was not to look for a synthetic Elizabethanism. 'We shall not save our souls by being Elizabethan.' To recreate the Globe would, he knew, be aesthetic anasthaesia, involving the audience in an insincere conspiracy to pretend that they were willing collaborators in a vain effort to turn the clock back. His answers to staging Shakespeare were similar to Brecht's for *his* plays and, in some senses, to

Chekhov's for his. He wanted scenery not to decorate and be literal, but to be expressive and metaphorical, and at the same time, in apparent contradiction, to be specific and be real, while being minimal and iconographic: the cart in *Mother Courage*, the nursery in *The Cherry Orchard*, the dining table in *The Voysey Inheritance*. 'To create a new hieroglyphic language of scenery. That, in a phrase, is the problem. If the designer finds himself competing with the actors, the sole interpreters Shakespeare has licensed, then it is he that is the intruder and must retire.'

In *The Prefaces* Granville Barker argues for a fluency of staging unbroken by scene changes. Likewise the verse should be spoken fast. 'Be swift, be swift, be not poetical,' he wrote on the dressing-room mirror of Cathleen Nesbitt when she played Perdita. Within the speed, however, detailed reality. *Meaning* above all.

It is the director's task, with the actors, to illuminate the meanings of a play: its vocabulary, its syntax, and its philosophy. The director has to ask what each scene is revealing about the characters and their actions: what story is each scene telling us? In *The Prefaces* Granville Barker exhumes, examines and explains the lost stagecraft of Shakespeare line by line, scene by scene, play by play.

Directing Shakespeare is a matter of understanding the meaning of a scene and staging it in the light of that knowledge. Easier said than done, but it's at the heart of the business of directing any play, and directing Shakespeare is merely directing writ large. Beyond that, as David Mamet has observed, 'choice of actions and adverbs constitute the craft of directing'. Get up from that chair and walk across the room. Slowly.

With Shakespeare as with any other playwright the director's job is to make the play live, now, in the present tense. 'Spontaneous enjoyment is the life of the theatre,' says Granville Barker in his Preface to *Love's Labour's Lost.* To receive a review, as Granville Barker did, headed *SHAKESPEARE ALIVE!* is the most, but should be the least, that a director must hope for.

I regard Granville Barker not only as the first modern English director but as the most influential. Curiously, partly as a 'result of his early withdrawal from the theatre, partly because his *Prefaces* have been out of print for many years, and partly because of his own self-effacement, he has been unjustly ignored both in the theatre and in the academic world, where the codification of their 'systems' has resulted in the canonisation of Brecht and Stanislavsky. I hope the re-publication of *The Prefaces* will right the balance. Granville Barker himself always thought of them as his permanent legacy to the theatre.

My sense of filial identification is not entirely a professional one. When I directed *The Voysey Inheritance* I wanted a photograph of the author on the poster. A number of people protested that it was the height, or depth, of vanity and self-aggrandisement to put my own photograph on the poster. I was astonished, I was bewildered, but I was not unflattered. I still can't see the resemblance, but it's not through lack of trying.

Two years ago the Royal National Theatre was presented with a wonderful bronze bust of Granville Barker by Katherine Scott (the wife, incidentally, of the Antarctic hero). For a while it sat on the windowsill of my office like a benign household god. Then it was installed on a bracket in the foyer opposite a bust of Olivier, the two men eyeing each other in wary mutual regard. A few months later it was stolen; an act of homage perhaps. I miss him.

Richard Eyre

Introduction

We have still much to learn about Shakespeare the playwright. Strange that it should be so, after three centuries of commentary and performance, but explicable. For the Procrustean methods of a changed theatre deformed the plays, and put the art of them to confusion; and scholars, with this much excuse, have been apt to divorce their Shakespeare from the theatre altogether, to think him a poet whose use of the stage was quite incidental, whose glory had small relation to it, for whose lapses it was to blame.

The Study and the Stage

THIS much is to be said for Garrick and his predecessors and successors in the practice of reshaping Shakespeare's work to the theatre of their time. The essence of it was living drama to them, and they meant to keep it alive for their public. They wanted to avoid whatever would provoke question and so check that spontaneity of response upon which acted drama depends. Garrick saw the plays, with their lack of 'art', through the spectacles of contemporary culture; and the bare Elizabethan stage, if it met his mind's eye at all, doubtless as a barbarous makeshift. Shakespeare was for him a problem; he tackled it, from our point of view, misguidedly and with an overplus of enthusiasm. His was a positive world; too near in time, moreover, as well as too opposed in taste to Shakespeare's to treat it perspectively. The romantic movement might have brought a more concordant outlook. But by then the scholars were off their own way; while the theatre began to think of its Shakespeare from the point of view of the picturesque, and, later, in terms of upholstery. Nineteenth-century drama developed along the lines of realistic illusion, and the staging of Shakespeare was further subdued to this, with inevitably disastrous effect on the speaking of his verse; there was less perversion of text perhaps, but actually more wrenching of the construction of the plays for the convenience of the stage carpenter. The public appetite for this sort of thing having been gorged, producers then turned to newer—and older—contrivances, leaving 're-alism' (so called) to the modern comedy that had fa-thered it. Amid much vaporous theorizing—but let us humbly own how hard it is not to write nonsense about art, which seems ever pleading to be enjoyed and not written about at all—the surprising discovery had been made that varieties of stagecraft and stage were not historical accidents but artistic obligations, that Greek drama belonged in a Greek theatre, that Elizabethan plays, therefore, would, presumably, do best upon an Elizabethan stage, that there was nothing sacrosanct about scenery, footlights, drop-curtain or any of their belongings. This brings us to the present situation.

There are few enough Greek theatres in which Greek tragedy can be played; few enough people want to see it, and they will applaud it encouragingly however it is done. Some acknowledgement is due to the altruism of the doers! Shakespeare is another matter. The English theatre, doubtful of its destiny, of necessity venal, open-ing its doors to all comers, seems yet, as by some instinct, to seek renewal of strength in him. An actor, unless success has made him cynical, or his talent be merely trivial, may take some pride in the hall mark of Shakes-pearean achievement. So may a manager if he thinks he can afford it. The public (or their spokesmen) seem to consider Shakespeare and his genius a sort of national property, which, truly, they do nothing to conserve, but in which they have moral rights not lightly to be flouted. The production of the plays is thus still apt to be marked by a timid respect for 'the usual thing'; their acting is crippled by pseudo-traditions, which are inert because they are not Shakespearean at all. They are the accumulation of two centuries of progressive misconception and distortion of his playwright's art. On the other hand, England has been spared production of Shakespeare according to this or that even more irrelevant theory of presentationalism, symbolism, constructivism or what not. There is the breach in the wall of 'realism', but we have not yet made up our minds to pass through, taking our Shakespeare with us.

Incidentally, we owe the beginning of the breach to Mr William Poel, who, with fanatical courage, when 'realism' was at the tottering height of its triumph in the later revivals of Sir Henry Irving, and the yet more richly upholstered revelations of Sir Herbert Tree, thrust the Elizabethan stage in all its apparent eccentricity upon our unwilling notice.[1] Mr Poel shook complacency. He could not expect to do much more; for he was a logical reformer. He showed us the Elizabethan stage, with Antony and Cleopatra, Troilus and Cressida, in their ruffs and farthingales as for Shakespeare's audiences they lived. Q.E.D. There, however, as far as the popular theatre was concerned, the matter seemed to rest for twenty years or so. But it was just such a demonstration that was needed; anything less drastic and provocative might have been passed over with mild approval.

To get the balance true, let us admit that while Shakespeare was an Elizabethan playwright he was—and now is to us—predominantly something much more. Therefore we had better not too unquestioningly thrust him back within the confines his genius has escaped, nor presume him to have felt the pettier circumstances of his theatre sacrosanct. Nor can we turn Elizabethans as we watch the plays; and every mental effort to do so will subtract from our enjoyment of them. This is the case against the circumstantial reproduction of Shakespeare's staging. But Mr Poel's achievement remains; he cleared for us from Shakespeare's stagecraft the scenic rubbish by which it had been so long encumbered and disguised. And we could now, if we would, make a promising fresh start. For the scholars, on their side, have lately—the scholarly among them—cut clear of the transcendental fog (scenic illusion of another sort) in which their nineteenth-century peers loved to lose themselves, and they too are beginning again at the beginning. A text acquires virtue now by its claim to be a prompt book, and the most comprehensive work of our time upon the Elizabethan stage is an elaborate sorting-out of plays, companies and theatres. On Dr Pollard's treatment of the texts and on the foundations of fact laid by Sir Edmund Chambers a new scholarship is rising, aiming first to see Shakespeare in the theatre for which he wrote. It is a scholarship, therefore, by which the theatre of today can profit, to which, by its acting of Shakespeare, it could contribute, one would hope. Nor should the scholars disdain the help; for criticism cannot live upon criticism, it needs refreshment from the living art. Besides, what is all the criticism and scholarship finally for if not to keep Shakespeare alive? And he must always be most alive—even if roughly and rudely alive—in the theatre. Let the scholars force a way in there, if need be. Its fervid atmosphere will do them good; the benefit will be mutual.

These Prefaces are an attempt to profit by this new scholarship and to contribute to it some research into Shakespeare's stagecraft, by examining the plays, one

after another, in the light of the interpretation he de-
signed for them, so far as this can be deduced; to discover,
if possible, the production he would have desired for
them, all merely incidental circumstances apart. They
might profit more written a generation hence, for the
ground they build upon is still far from clear. And this
introduction is by no means a conspectus of the subject;
that can only come as a sequel. There has been, in this
branch of Shakespearean study, too much generalization
and far too little analysis of material.[2]

Shakespeare's Stagecraft

SHAKESPEARE'S own career was not a long one. The
whole history of the theatre he wrote for does not cover
a century. Between Marlowe and Massinger, from the
first blaze to the glowing of the embers, it is but fifty
years. Yet even while Shakespeare was at work, the stage
to which he fitted his plays underwent constant and
perhaps radical change. From Burbage's first theatre to
the Globe, then to Blackfriars, not to mention excursions
to Court and into the great halls—change of audiences
and their behaviour, of their taste, development of the
art of acting, change of the stage itself and its resources
were all involved in the progress, and are all, we may
be sure, reflected to some degree in the plays themselves.
We guess at the conditions of each sort of stage and
theatre, but there is often the teasing question to which
of them had a play, as we have it now, been adapted.
And of the 'private' theatre, most in vogue for the ten
years preceding the printing of the First Folio so far we
know least. The dating of texts and their ascription to
the usages of a particular theatre may often be a search-
light upon their stagecraft. Here is much work for the
new scholarship.

Conversely, the watchful working-out of the plays in action upon this stage or that would be of use to the scholars, who otherwise must reconstruct their theatre and gloss their texts as in a vacuum. The play was once fitted to the stage; it is by no means impossible to rebuild that stage now, with its doors, balconies, curtains and machines, by measuring the needs of the play. It is idle, for instance, to imagine scenes upon inner or upper stage without evidence that they will be audible or visible there; and editing is still vitiated by lack of this simple knowledge. Here, if nowhere else, this present research must fall short, for its method should rightly be experimental; more than one mind should be at work on it, moreover.

The text of a play is a score waiting performance, and the performance and its preparation are, almost from the beginning, a work of collaboration. A producer may direct the preparation, certainly. But if he only knows how to give orders, he has mistaken his vocation; he had better be a drill-sergeant. He might talk to his company when they all met together for the first time to study *Love's Labour's Lost, Julius Cæsar* or *King Lear*, on some such lines as these Prefaces pursue, giving a considered opinion of the play, drawing a picture of it in action, providing, in fact, a hypothesis which mutual study would prove—and might partly disprove. No sort of study of a play can better the preparation of its performance if this is rightly done. The matured art of the playwright lies in giving life to characters in action, and the secret of it in giving each character a due chance in the battle, the action of a play becoming literally the fighting of a battle of character. So the greater the playwright, the wider and deeper his sympathies, the more genuine this opposition will be and the less easily will a single mind grasp it, as it must be grasped, in the fullness of its emotion. The dialogue of a play runs—and often intricately—upon lines of reason, but it is charged besides with an emotion which speech releases, yet only releases fully when the speaker is—as an actor is—identified with the character. There is further the incidental action, implicit in the dialogue, which springs to life only when a scene is in being. A play, in fact, as we find it written, is a magic spell; and even the magician cannot always foresee the full effect of it.

Not every play, it must be owned, will respond to such intensive study. Many, ambitiously conceived, would collapse under the strain. Many are mere occasions for display of their actors' wit or eloquence, good looks or nice behaviour, and meant to be no more; and if they are skilfully contrived the parts fit together and the whole machine should go like clockwork. Nor, in fact, are even the greatest plays often so studied. There is hardly a theatre in the world where masterpiece and trumpery alike are not rushed through rehearsals to an arbitrarily effective performance, little more learned of them than the words, gaps in the understanding of them filled up with 'business'—effect without cause, the demand for this being the curse of the theatre as of other arts, as of other things than art. Not to such treatment will the greater plays of Shakespeare yield their secrets. But working upon a stage which reproduced the essential conditions of his, working as students, not as showmen merely, a company of actors might well find many of the riddles of the library answering themselves unasked. And these Prefaces could best be a record of such work, if such work were to be done.

We cannot, on the other hand, begin our research by postulating the principles of the Elizabethan stage. One is tempted to say it had none, was too much a child of nature to bother about such things. Principles were doubtless imposed upon it when it reached respectability, and heads would be bowed to the yoke. Shakespeare's among them? He had served a most practical apprenticeship to his trade. If he did not hold horses at the door, he sat behind the curtains, we may be sure, and held the prompt book on occasion. He acted, he cobbled other men's plays, he could write his own to order. Such a one may stay a journeyman if he is not a genius, but he will not become a doctrinaire. Shakespeare's work shows such principles as the growth of a tree shows. It is not haphazard merely because it is not formal; it is shaped by inner strength. The theatre, as he found it, allowed him and encouraged him to great freedom of development. Because the material resources of a stage are simple, it does not follow that the technique of its playwriting will stay so. Crude work may show up more crudely, when there are none of the fal-lals of illusion to disguise it that the modern theatre provides. But, if he has it in him, a dramatist can, so unfettered, develop the essentials of his art more boldly and more subtly too. The Elizabethan drama made an amazingly quick advance from crudity to an excellence which was often technically most elaborate. The advance and the not less amazing gulf which divides its best from its worst may be ascribed to the simplicity of the machinery it employed. That its decadence was precipitated by the influence of the Masque and the shifting of its centre of interest from the barer public stage to the candle-lit private theatre, where the machinery of the Masque became effective, it would be rash to assert; but the occurrences are suspiciously related. Man and machine (here at any rate is a postulate, if a platitude!) are false allies in the theatre, secretly at odds; and when man gets the worst of it, drama is impoverished; and the struggle, we may add, is perennial. No great drama depends upon pageantry. All great drama tends to concentrate upon character; and, even so, not upon picturing men as they show themselves to the world like figures on a stage—though that is how it must ostensibly show them—but on the hidden man. And the progress of Shakespeare's art from *Love's Labour's Lost* to *Hamlet*, and thereafter with a difference, lies in the simplifying of this paradox and the solving of the problem it presents; and the process involves the developing of a very subtle sort of stagecraft indeed.

For one result we have what we may call a very self-contained drama. Its chief values, as we know, have not changed with the fashions of the theatre. It relies much on the music of the spoken word, and a company of schoolchildren with pleasant voices, and an ear for rhythm, may vociferate through a play to some effect. It is as much to be enjoyed in the reading, if we hear it in imagination as we read, as drama meant to be acted can be. As with its simplicities then, so it should be, we presume, with its complexities. The subtly emotional use of verse and the interplay of motive and character, can these not be appreciated apart from the bare boards of their original setting? It does not follow. It neither follows that the advantages of the Elizabethan stage were wholly negative nor that, with our present knowledge, we can imagine the full effect of a play in action upon it. The imagining of a play in action is, under no circumstances, an easy thing.[3] What would one not give to go backward through the centuries to see the first performance of *Hamlet*, played as Shakespeare had it played![4] In default, if we could but make ourselves read it as if it were a manuscript fresh from its author's hands! There is much to be said for turning one's back on the editors, even, when possible, upon the First Folio with its demarcation of acts and scenes, in favour of the Quartos—Dr Pollard's 'good' Quartos—in their yet greater simplicity.

The Convention of Place

IT is, for instance, hard to discount the impression made merely by reading: *Scene i—Elsinore. A platform before the Castle*; and most of us have, to boot, early memories of painted battlements and tenth-century castles (of ageing Hamlets and their portly mothers for that matter) very difficult to dismiss. No great harm, one protests; it was a help, perhaps, to the unimaginative. But it is a first step to the certain misunderstanding of Shakespeare's stagecraft. The 'if, how and when' of the presenting of localities on the Elizabethan stage is, of course, a complex question. Shakespeare himself seems to have followed, consciously, no principles in the matter, nor was his practice very logical, nor at all consistent. It may vary with the play he is writing and the particular stage he is writing for; it will best be studied in relation to each play. We can, however, free ourselves from one general misconception which belongs to our own over-logical standpoint. When we learn with a shock of surprise—having begun in the schoolroom upon the Shakespeare of the editors, it comes as belated news to us—that neither battlements, throne rooms nor picturesque churchyards were to be seen at the Globe, and that *Elsinore. A platform before the Castle* is not Shakespeare at all, we yet imagine ourselves among the audience there busily conjuring these things up before the eye of faith. The Elizabethan audience was at no such pains. Nor was this their alternative to seeing the actors undisguisedly concerned with the doors, curtains and balconies which, by the play's requirements, should have been anything but what they were. As we, when a play has no hold on us, may fall to thinking about the scenery, so to a Globe audience, unmoved, the stage might be an obvious bare stage. But are we conscious of the scenery behind the actor when the play really moves us? If we are, there is something very wrong with the scenery, which should know its place as a background. The audience was not conscious of curtain and balcony when Burbage played Hamlet to them. They were conscious of Hamlet. That conventional background faded as does our painted illusion, and they certainly did not deliberately conjure up in its place mental pictures of Elsinore. The genus audience is passive, if expectant, imaginatively lazy till roused, never, one may be sure, at pains to make any effort that is generally unnecessary to enjoyment.

With Shakespeare the locality of a scene has dramatic importance, or it has none; and this is as true of his early plays as his late ones. Both in *Richard II* and *Antony and Cleopatra*, scene after scene passes with no exact indication of where we may be. With *Cleopatra* we are surely in Egypt, with Cæsar in Rome. Pompey appears, and the talk tells us that both Egypt and Rome are elsewhere; but positively where Pompey is at the moment we never learn.[5] Indoors or outdoors? The action of the scene or the clothing of the characters will tell us this if we need to know. But, suddenly transported to the Parthian war, our whereabouts is made amply plain. It is, however, made plain by allusion. The information peeps out through talk of kindred things; we are hardly aware we are being told, and, again, we learn no more than we need to learn. This, truly, is a striking development from the plump and plain

> Barkloughly Castle call they this at hand?

of Richard II, even from the more descriptive

> I am a stranger here in Gloucestershire:
> These high wild hills and rough, uneven ways
> Draw out our miles...

by which Shakespeare pictures and localizes the manoeuvres of Richard and Bolingbroke when he wants to.
But the purpose is the same, and the method essentially
the same.[6] Towards the end of the later play come scene
after scene of the marching and countermarching of
armies, of fighting, of truce, all the happenings of three
days' battle. Acts III and IV contain twenty-eight scenes
long and short; some of them are very short; three of
them have but four lines apiece. The editors conscien-
tiously ticket them *A plain near Actium, Another part of the
plain, Another part of the plain* and so on, and conclude that
Shakespeare is really going too far and too fast, is indeed
(I quote Sir Edmund Chambers) 'in some danger of
outrunning the apprehensions of his auditory.' Indeed he
might be if this cinematographic view of his intentions
were the right one! But it utterly falsifies them. Show an
audience such a succession of painted scenes—if you
could at the pace required—and they would give attention to nothing else whatever; the drama would pass
unnoticed. Had Shakespeare tried to define the whereabouts of every scene in any but the baldest phrases—the
protesting editors seem not to see that he makes no
attempt to; only *they* do!—he would have had to lengthen
and complicate them; had he written only a labelling
line or two he would still have distracted his audience
from the essential drama. Ignoring whereabouts, letting
it at most transpire when it naturally will, the characters
capture all attention. This is the true gain of the bare
stage; unless to some dramatic end no precious words
need be spent, in complying with the undramatic demands of space and time; incarnation of character can
be all in all. Given such a crisis as this the gain is yet
greater. We are carried through the phases of the three
days' battle; and what other stage convention would
allow us so varied a view of it, could so isolate the true

drama of it? For do we not pass through such a crisis in reality with just that indifference to time and place? These scenes, in their kind, show Shakespeare's stage-craft, not at its most reckless, but at its very best, and exemplify perfectly the freedom he enjoyed that the stage of visual illusion has inevitably lost. His drama is attached solely to its actors and their acting; that, perhaps, puts it in a phrase. They carry place and time with them as they move. The modern theatre still accepts the convention that measures time more or less by a play's convenience; a half-hour stands for an hour or more, and we never question the vagary. It was no more strange to an Elizabethan audience to see a street in Rome turned, in the use made of it, to the Senate House by the drawing of a curtain and the disclosure of Cæsar's state, to find Cleopatra's Monument now on the upper stage because Antony had to be drawn up to it, later on the lower because Cleopatra's death-scene could best be played there; it would seem that they were not too astonished even when Juliet, having taken leave of Romeo on the balcony of her bedroom and watched him descend to the lower stage, the scene continuing, came down, a few lines later, to the lower stage herself, bringing, so to speak, her bedroom with her—since this apparently is what she must have done.[7] For neither Senate House, Monument nor balcony had rights and reality of their own. They existed for the convenience of the actors, whose touch gave them life, a shadowy life at most; neglected, they existed no longer.[8]

Shakespeare's stagecraft concentrates, and inevitably, upon opportunity for the actor. We think now of the plays themselves; their first public knew them by their acting; and the development of the actor's art from the agilities and funniments of the clown, and from round-mouthed rhetoric to imaginative interpreting of character by such standards as Hamlet set up for his players, was a factor in the drama's triumph that we now too often ignore. Shakespeare himself, intent more and more upon plucking out the heart of the human mystery, stimulated his actors to a poignancy and intimacy of emotional expression—still can stimulate them to it—as no other playwright has quite learned to do.

The Speaking of the Verse

His verse was, of course, his chief means to this emotional expression; and when it comes to staging the plays, the speaking of verse must be the foundation of all study. The changes of three hundred years have of themselves put difficulties in our way here; though there are some besides—as one imagines—of Shakespeare's own making. Surely his syntax must now and then have puzzled even his contemporaries. Could they have made much more than we can of Leontes'

> Affection! thy intention stabs the centre;
> Thou dost make possible things not so held,
> Communicat'st with dreams;—How can this be?
> With what's unreal thou coactive art,
> And fellow'st nothing; then, 'tis very credent
> Thou may'st co-join with something; and thou dost;
> And that beyond commission; and I find it,
> And that to the infection of my brains,
> And hardening of my brows.

The confusion of thought and intricacy of language is dramatically justified. Shakespeare is picturing a genuinely jealous man (the sort of man that Othello was *not*) in the grip of a mental epilepsy. We parse the passage and dispute its sense; spoken, as it was meant to be, in a choking torrent of passion, probably a modicum of sense slipped through, and its first hearers did not find it a mere rigmarole. But we are apt to miss even that much. Other passages, of early and late writing, may always have had as much sound as sense to them; but now, to the casual hearer, they will convey more sound than sense by far. Nor do puns mean to us what they meant to the Elizabethans, delighting in their language for its own sake. Juliet's tragic fantasia upon 'Aye' and 'I' sounds all but ridiculous, and one sympathizes with an actress hesitating to venture on it. How far, apart from the shifting of accents and the recolouring of vowels, has not the whole habit of English speech changed in these three hundred years? In the theatre it was slowing down, one fancies, throughout the eighteenth century; and in the nineteenth, as far as Shakespeare was concerned, it grew slower and slower, till on occasions one thought—even hoped—that shortly the actor would stop altogether. There may have been more than one cause; imitation of the French Augustans, the effort to make antiquated phrases understood, the increasing size of the theatres themselves would all contribute to it. The result, in any case, is disastrous. Elizabethan drama was built upon vigour and beauty of speech. The groundlings may often have deserved Shakespeare's strictures, but they would stand in discomfort for an hour or so to be stirred by the sound of verse. Some of the actors no doubt were robustious periwig-pated fellows, but, equally, it was no empty ideal of acting he put into Hamlet's mouth—and Burbage's. We may suppose that at its best the mere speaking of the plays was a very brilliant thing, compared to *bel canto*, or to a pianist's virtuosity. The emotional appeal of our modern music was in it, and it could be tested by ears trained to the rich and delicate fretwork of the music of that day. Most Hamlets—not being playwrights—make a mild joke of telling us they'd as lief the town-crier spoke their lines, but we may hear in it the echo of some of Shakespeare's sorest trials.

The speaking of his verse must be studied, of course, in relation to the verse's own development. The actor must not attack its supple complexities in *Antony and Cleopatra* and *Cymbeline*, the mysterious dynamics of *Macbeth*, the nobilities of *Othello*, its final pastoral simplicities in *A Winter's Tale* and *The Tempest* without preliminary training in the lyricism, the swift brilliance and the masculine clarity of the earlier plays. A modern actor, alas, thinks it simple enough to make his way, splay-footed, through

> The cloud-capped towers, the gorgeous palaces...

though Berowne's

> I, forsooth, in love...

or one of Oberon's apostrophes will defeat him utterly. And, without an ear trained to the delicacy of the earlier work, his hearers, for their part, will never know how shamefully he is betraying the superb ease of the later. If we are to make Shakespeare our own again we must all be put to a little trouble about it. We must recapture as far as may be his lost meanings; and the sense of a phrase we *can* recapture, though instinctive emotional response to it may be a loss forever. The tunes that he writes to, the whole great art of his music-making, we can master. Actors can train their ears and tongues and can train our ears to it. We talk of lost arts. No art is ever lost while the means to it survive. Our faculties rust by disuse and by misuse are coarsened, but they quickly recover delight in a beautiful thing. Here, at any rate, is the touchstone by which all interpreting of Shakespeare the playwright must first—and last—be tried.

The Boy-Actress

MORE than one of the conditions of his theatre made this medium of accomplished speech of such worth to him. Boys played the women parts; and what could a boy bring to Juliet, Rosalind or Cleopatra beyond grace of manner and charm of speech? We have been used to women on the stage for two hundred and fifty years or more, and a boy Juliet—if the name on the programme revealed one, for nothing else might—would seem an odd fish to us; no one would risk a squeaking Cleopatra; though, as for Rosalind, through three-parts of the play a boy would have the best of it. But the parts were written for boys; not, therefore, without consideration of how boys could act them most convincingly. Hence, of course, the popularity of the heroine so disguised. The disguise was perfect; the make-believe one degree more complex, certainly, than it needs to be with us; but once you start make-believe it matters little how far you go with it; there is, indeed, some enjoyment in the make-believe itself. But, further, it is Shakespeare's constant care to demand nothing of a boy-actress that might turn to unseemliness or ridicule. He had not much taste for what is called 'domestic drama,' nor does he dose us very heavily with Doll Tearsheet, Mistress Overdone and their like. Constance mourns Arthur's loss, Lady Macduff has her little son, but no mother croons over the child in her arms. Paulina brings Hermione's baby to Leontes, it is true; but see with what tact, from this point of view, the episode is managed. And love-scenes are most carefully contrived. Romeo and Juliet are seldom alone together; never for long, but in the balcony-scene; and in this, the most famous of love-scenes, they are kept from all contact with each other. Consider *Antony and*

Cleopatra. Here is a tragedy of sex without one single scene of sexual appeal. That aspect of Cleopatra is reflected for us in talk about her; mainly by Enobarbus, who is not mealymouthed; but his famed description of her voluptuousness is given us when she has been out of our sight for several scenes. The play opens with her parting from Antony, and in their two short encounters we see her swaying him by wit, malice and with the moods of her mind. Not till the story takes its tragic plunge and sex is drowned in deeper passion are they ever intimately together; till he is brought to her dying there has been occasion for but one embrace. Contrast this with a possible Cleopatra planned to the advantage of the actress of today.

Shakespeare, artist that he was, turned this limitation to account, made loss into a gain.[9] Feminine charm—of which the modern stage makes such capital—was a medium denied him. So his men and women encounter upon a plane where their relation is made rarer and intenser by poetry, or enfranchised in a humour which surpasses more primitive love-making. And thus, perhaps, he was helped to discover that the true stuff of tragedy and of the liveliest comedy lies beyond sensual bounds. His studies of women seem often to be begun from some spiritual paces beyond the point at which a modern dramatist leaves off. Curious that not a little of the praise lavished upon the beauty and truth of them— mainly by women—may be due to their having been written to be played by boys!

Much could be said for the restoring of the celibate stage; but the argument, one fears, would be academic. Here, though, is practical counsel. Let the usurping actress remember that her sex is a liability, not an asset. The dramatist of today may refuse to exploit its allurements, but may legitimately allow for the sympathetic effect of it; though the less he does so, perhaps, the better for his play and the more gratitude the better sort of actress will show him. But Shakespeare makes no such demands, has left no blank spaces for her to fill with her charm. He asks instead for self-forgetful clarity of perception, and for a sensitive, spirited, athletic beauty of speech and conduct, which will leave prettiness and its lures at a loss, and the crudities of more Circean appeal looking very crude indeed.

The Soliloquy

THIS convention of the boy-actress may be said to give a certain remoteness to a play's acting. The soliloquy brings a compensating intimacy, and its use was an important part of Shakespeare's stagecraft. Its recognized usefulness was for the disclosing of the plot, but he soon improved upon this. Soliloquy becomes the means by which he brings us not only to a knowledge of the more secret thoughts of his characters, but into the closest emotional touch with them too. Here the platform stage helped him, as the stage of scenic illusion now defeats his purpose. But it is not altogether a question of 'realism' and the supposed obligation this lays upon a real man in a real-looking room to do nothing he would not do if the whole affair were real.

There is no escape from convention in the theatre, and all conventions can be made acceptable, though they cannot all be used indiscriminately, for they are founded in the physical conditions of the stage of their origin and are often interdependent one with another. Together they form a code, and they are as a treaty made with the audience. No article of it is to be abrogated unless we can be persuaded to consent, and upon its basis we surrender our imaginations to the playwright.

With the soliloquy upon the platform stage it is a case—as so often where convention is concerned—of extremes meeting. There is no illusion, so there is every illusion. Nothing very strange about this man, not even the dress he wears, leaning forward a little we could touch him; we are as intimate and familiar with him as it is possible to be. We agree to call him 'Hamlet', to suppose that he is where he says he is, we admit that he thinks aloud and in blank verse too. It is possible that the more we are asked to imagine the easier we find it to do. It is certain that, once our imagination is working, visual illusion will count for little in the stimulating of emotion beside this intimacy that allows the magnetism of personality full play.

There is no more important task for the producer of Shakespeare than to restore to the soliloquy its rightful place in a play's economy, and in particular to regain for it full emotional effect. We now accept the convention frigidly, the actor manoeuvres with it timidly. Banished behind footlights into that other world of illusion, the solitary self-communing figure rouses our curiosity at best. Yet further adapted to the self-contained methods of modern acting, the soliloquy has quite inevitably become a slack link in the play's action, when it should be a recurring reinforcement to its strength. Shakespeare never pinned so many dramatic fortunes to a merely utilitarian device. Time and again he may be feeling his way through a scene for a grip on his audience, and it is the soliloquy ending it that will give him—and his actor—the stranglehold. When he wishes to quicken the pulse of the action, to screw up its tension in a second or so, the soliloquy serves him well. For a parallel to its full effectiveness on Shakespeare's stage we should really look to the modern music-hall comedian getting on terms with his audience. We may measure the response to Burbage's

O, that this too too solid flesh would melt . . .

by recalling—those of us that happily can—Dan Leno as a washerwoman, confiding domestic troubles to a theatre full of friends, and taken unhindered to their hearts. The problem is not really a difficult one. If we solve the physical side of it by restoring, in essentials, the relation between actor and audience that the intimacy of the platform stage provided, the rest should soon solve itself.

Costume

THE problem of costume, when it arises, is a subtler one; nor probably is it capable of any logical solution. Half the plays can be quite appropriately dressed in the costume of Shakespeare's own time. It is a false logic which suggests that to match their first staging we should dress them in the costume of ours. For with costume goes custom and manners—or the lack of them. It may be both a purge and a tonic to the sluggish-fancied spectator to be shown a Prince of Denmark in coat and trousers and a Grave-digger in a bowler hat, for reminder that here is a play, not a collection of ritualized quotations. But physic is for the sick; also, there may be less drastic cures. When archaeology took hold upon the nineteenth-century mind it became a matter of moment to lodge Hamlet in historic surroundings; and withers were wrung by the anachronisms of ducats and a murder of Gonzago, French rapiers and the rest. A needlessly teasing difficulty; why reproduce it in terms of a young man in a dinner jacket searching for a sword—a thing not likely to be lying about in his modern mother's sitting room—with which to kill Polonius, who certainly has window curtains to hide behind instead of arras? This gain of intimacy—with a Hamlet we might find sitting opposite at a dinner party—may well be a gain in sympathy. It was originally a great gain, a gift to Shakespeare's audience. But we pay too high a price for it.

What was the actual Elizabethan practice in this matter of costuming is not comprehensively known. We can only say safely that, as with other matters, it was neither constant, consistent, nor, from our present point of view, rational. It was based upon the use of the clothes of the time; but these might be freely and fantastically adapted to suit a particular play or advantage some character in it. Dramatic effect was probably the first consideration and the last. There were such fancy dresses as Oberon or Puck or Caliban might wear; there was always the symbolizing of royalty, and a king would wear a crown whenever he could; there was the utility of knowing Romans from Britons by sight in *Cymbeline*, the martial Roman from the effete Egyptian in *Antony and Cleopatra*, and a Scottish lord when you saw him in *Macbeth*, if we may judge by Malcolm's comment upon Rosse's appearance:

> My countryman; and yet I know him not.

Our difficulty, of course, arises mainly over the historical plays. Not over the English Histories, even so; we can dress Richard III or Henry V by the light of our own superior knowledge of what they wore, and never find it clash violently with anything Shakespeare has put on their backs or in their mouths. But when we come to Julius Cæsar plucking open his doublet, to the conspirators against him with their hats about their ears, and to Cleopatra's

> Cut my lace, Charmian.

not to mention British Imogen in her doublet and hose, we must stop and consider.

The common practice is, in these instances, to ignore the details of Shakespeare's text altogether; to dress Cæsar in his toga, Cleopatra in her habit as she lived, with never a stay-lace about her (though, truly, the costumier, let alone, will tend to get his fashion a few thousand years wrong and turn her out more like the wife of Tutankhamen); and as to Imogen and her surroundings, we do our best to compromise with skins and woad. This may be a lesser evil than presenting a Cæsar recalling Sir Walter Raleigh and a Cleopatra who would make us think of Mary Queen of Scots, but it is no solution of the problem. For the actors have to speak these lines, and if action and appearance contradict them, credibility is destroyed. And the constant credibility of the actor must be a producer's first care. Nor is this all, nor is it, perhaps, the most important thing to consider. The plays are full of reference, direct and indirect, to Elizabethan custom. They are, further, impregnated with what we call 'Renaissance feeling', some more, some less, but all to a degree. Now of this last we have a sense which is likelier to be a better help to their appreciation than any newfangled knowledge of the correct cut of Cleopatra's clothes will be! We know Iago for a Machiavellian figure (so called), and miss none of Shakespeare's intention. But if ever two men breathed the air of a sixteenth-century court, Hamlet and Claudius of Denmark do, and to relate them in habit and behaviour to the twilight figures of Saxo Grammaticus is as much a misinterpretation as any mauling of the text can be. They exist essentially doubtless—as do all the major characters of the plays—in their perennial humanity. But never let us forget the means by which this deeper truth of them is made vivid and actual. There have been better intellects than Shakespeare's, and poetry as good as his. He holds his supreme place by his dramatist's necessary power of bringing thought and vague emotion to the terms of action and convincing speech; further, and far more than is often allowed, by his peculiar gift of bringing into contribution the common-place traffic of life. However wide the spoken word may range, there must be the actor, anchored to the stage. However high, then, with Shakespeare, the thought or emotion may soar, we shall always find the transcendental set in the familiar. He keeps this balance constantly adjusted; and, at his play's greatest moments, when he must make most sure of our response, he will employ the simplest means. The higher arguments of the plays are thus kept always within range, and their rooted humanity blossoms in a fertile upspringing of expressive little things. Neglect or misinterpret these, the inner wealth of Shakespeare will remain, no doubt, and we may mine for it, but we shall have levelled his landscape bare.

Shakespeare's own attitude in this matter of costume and customs was as inconsistent as his practice was casual. He knew what *his* Cæsar or Cleopatra would be wearing and would casually drop in a reference to it. Yet the great Romans themselves were aliens to him. The great idea of Rome fired his imagination. Brutus, Cassius and Antony do not turn typical Elizabethan gentlemen; and to the end of that play he is striving to translate Plutarch. Whenever, on the other hand, even for a moment he has made a character all his own, he cannot but clothe it in lively familiar detail. Cleopatra's are the coquetries of a great lady of his own time, in their phrasing, in the savour. When the heights of the tragedy have to be scaled, manners will not so much matter. But if we make her, at the play's beginning, a pseudo-classic, languishing Oriental, we must do it in spite of Shakespeare, not by his help. What then is the solution of this problem, if the sight of the serpent of old Nile in a farthingale will too dreadfully offend us? We can compromise. Look at Tintoretto's and Paolo Veronese's paintings of 'classic' subjects. We accept them readily enough.

Sometimes, within the boundaries of a play, the centuries seem all at odds. *Cymbeline* need not trouble us, its Roman Britain is pure 'once upon a time'. But in *King Lear*, for instance, Shakespeare is at unwonted pains to throw us back into some heathen past. Yet Edmund is another Iago, Edgar might have been at Wittenberg with Hamlet, and Oswald steps straight from the seventeenth-century London streets. Here, though, the dominant barbarism is the important thing; the setting for Goneril and Regan, Lear's tyranny and madness, and Gloucester's blinding. To a seventeenth-century audience Oswald was so identifiable a figure that it would not matter greatly how he dressed; the modern designer of costume must show him up as best he may. Each play, in fine, if it presents a problem at all, presents its own.

The Integrity of the Text

THE text, one says at first blush, can present no problem at all. The plays should be acted as Shakespeare wrote them—how dispute it? They should be; and it is as well, before we discuss hard cases, to have the principle freely admitted. Lip service enough is done it nowadays, and Colley Cibber's *Richard III*, Tate's *Lear* and Garrick's improvements are at the back of our bookshelves, but we still find Messrs John Doe and Richard Roe slicing out lines by the dozen and even a scene or so, or chopping and changing them to suit their scenery. This will not do. Shakespeare was not a perfect playwright; there can be no such thing. Nor did he aim at a mechanical perfection, but a vitality, and this he achieved. At best then, we cut and carve the body of a play to its peril. It may be robustly, but it may be very delicately organized. And we still know little enough of the laws of its existence, and some of us, perhaps, are not such very skilful surgeons; nor is any surgeon to be recommended who operates for his own convenience.

This good rule laid down, what are the exceptions that go to prove it? There is the pornographic difficulty. This is not such a stumbling block to us as it was to Bowdler, to some bright young eyes nowadays it is quite imperceptible, in fact. Yet, saving their presence, it exists; for it exists aesthetically. Shakespeare's characters often make obscene jokes. The manners of his time permitted it. The public manners of ours still do not. Now the dramatic value of a joke is to be measured by its effect upon an audience, and each is meant to make its own sort of effect. If then, instead of giving them a passing moment's amusement, it makes a thousand people uncomfortable and for the next five minutes very self-conscious, it fails of its true effect. This argument must not be stretched to cover the silliness of turning 'God' into 'Heaven' and of making Othello call Desdemona a 'wanton' (the practice, as I recollect, of the eighteen-nineties), nor to such deodorizing of *Measure for Measure* that it becomes hard to discover what all the fuss is about. If an audience cannot think of Angelo and the Duke, Pompey and Lucio, Isabella and Mistress Overdone, and themselves to boot, as fellow-creatures all, the play is not for them. Othello must call Desdemona a 'whore', and let those that do not like it leave the theatre; what have such queasy minds to do with the pity and terror of her murder and his death? Again, to make Beatrice so mealymouthed that she may not tell us how the devil is to meet her at the gates of hell, 'like an old cuckold with horns on his head', is to dress her in a crinoline, not a farthingale. But suppression of a few of the more scabrous jokes will not leave a play much the poorer; nor, one may add, will the average playgoer be much the wiser or merrier for hearing them, since they are often quite hard to understand.

Topical passages are a similar difficulty. With their savour, if not their very meaning lost, they show like dead wood in the living tree of the dialogue and are better, one would suppose, cut away. But no hard and fast rule will apply. Macbeth's porter's farmer and equivocator will never win spontaneous laughter again. But we cannot away with them, or nothing is left of the porter. Still the baffled low comedian must not, as his wont is, obscure the lines with bibulous antics. There will be that little dead spot in the play, and nothing can be done about it. Rosencrantz' reference to the 'eyrie of children' is meaningless except to the student. Is the play the poorer for the loss of it? But the logic that will take this out had better not rob us of

> Dead shepherd, now I find thy saw of might;
> Who ever loved that loved not at first sight?

And there is the strange case of

The lady of the Strachy married the yeoman of the wardrobe.

Nobody knows what it means, but everybody finds it funny when it is spoken in its place. And this has its parallels.

In general, however, better play the plays as we find them. The blue pencil is a dangerous weapon; and its use grows on a man, for it solves too many little difficulties far too easily.

Lastly, for a golden rule, whether staging or costuming or cutting is in question, and a comprehensive creed, a producer might well pin this on his wall: Gain Shakespeare's effects by Shakespeare's means when you can; for, plainly, this will be the better way. But gain Shakespeare's effects; and it is your business to discern them.

1927

Notes

1   But it should not be forgotten that Sir Herbert Tree, happy in the orthodoxy of public favour, welcomed the heretic Mr Poel more than once to a share in his Shakespeare Festivals.

2   I do not deal in general therefore with certain vexed questions, such as act-division, which still need to be looked at, I think, in the light of the particular play.

3   I remember a most intelligent reader of a modern play missing the whole point of a scene through which the chief character was to sit conspicuously and eloquently silent. He counted only with the written dialogue. I remember, when I thought I knew *King Lear* well enough, being amazed at the effect, all dialogue apart, of the mere meeting, when I saw it, of blind Gloucester and mad Lear.

4   Though, in a sense, there was no first performance of *Hamlet*. And doubtless many of the audience for Shakespeare's new version of the old play only thought he had spoiled a good story of murder and revenge by adding too much talk to it.

5   Unless it may be said that we learn in the scene after whereabouts he *was*.

6   And in *Coriolanus*, which probably postdates *Antony and Cleopatra*, with Marcius' 'A goodly city is this Antium,' we are back to the barely informative. It serves Shakespeare's purpose; he asks no more.

7   I fancy, though, that the later Shakespeare would have thought this a clumsy device.

8   How far this is true of other dramatists than Shakespeare I do not pretend to say; nor how far, with him, the influence of the private theatre, making undoubtedly towards the scenic stage

and (much later) for illusion, did not modify his practice, when he had that stage to consider. A question, again, for the bibliographers and historians.

9 There is no evidence, of course, that he felt it a loss, no such reference to the insufficiency of the boy-actress as there is to the overself-sufficiency of the clown. Women did appear in the Masques, if only to dance, so the gulf to be bridged was not a broad one. But the Elizabethan was as shocked by the notion of women appearing upon the public stage as the Chinese playgoer is today.

Coriolanus

CORIOLANUS cannot be ranked with the greatest of the tragedies. It lacks their transcendent vitality and metaphysical power. But while neither story nor characters evoke such qualities, those they do evoke are here in full measure. The play is notable for its craftsmanship. It is the work of a man who knows what the effect of each stroke will be, and wastes not one of them. And while ease and simplicity may sometimes be lacking, an uncertain or superfluous speech it would be hard to find. Was Shakespeare perhaps aware of some ebbing of his imaginative vitality—well there may have been after the creation in about as many years of *Othello*, *King Lear*, *Antony and Cleopatra* and *Macbeth*! and did he purposefully choose a subject and characters which he could make the most of by judgment and skill?

The play follows close, it would seem, upon *Antony and Cleopatra*. Between the two there is the general likeness of a setting in Roman history. For the rest, the contrasts are so many and so marked as hardly to be fortuitous. To that large picture of an imperial Rome and a decadent Egypt and of

> The triple pillar of the world transformed
> Into a strumpet's fool.

succeeds this story of earlier and austerer days, of a Rome still challengeable by her neighbours, and of a very different hero. Antony and Caius Marcius are men of action both. But Antony is the astute politician too, and by that talent could save himself from disaster if he would—does save himself and has the game in his hands, only to throw it away because

The beds i' the East are soft.

Antony—and Othello and Macbeth too—are soldiers, famous generals; but that is not the side of them we come to know. Coriolanus is the man of action seen in action, and among the heroes of the maturer canon unique in this.[1] He is the younger man, a fighter and a brilliant one, but effectively no more. He is at heart— and despite his trials remains to the end—the incorrigible boy, with 'Boy!' for the final insult flung at him by Aufidius that he will at no price swallow. And save in physical valour (of which in the elder, by the plan of the action, we hear but see nothing) in every trait he and Antony radically differ. To the one his men are 'my good fellows'. He jokes with them, praises them impulsively and generously for their pluck. The other is curt, even to friends and equals, self-conscious, and incapable of the least appeal to the populace he despises. In his contempt for spoils and rewards, in his stubbornness, his aristocratic pride, in his chastity—Virgilia greeting him on his minatory return, it is

> Now, by the jealous queen of heaven, that kiss
> I carried from thee, dear; and my true lip
> Hath virgined it ever since.

—in every significant feature the two stand contrasted.

Then in Cleopatra's place we have Volumnia; for the exotic mistress the Roman mother. Yet each in her fashion brings ruin, to lover or son. And for the Egyptian Court, in which, says Enobarbus,

> Mine and most of our fortunes to-night shall be—drunk to bed.

we exchange that picture of the simple Roman home, its great ladies content to *set themselves down on two low stools and sew.*

The contrasts are pervasive too. In the one play the action is spacious and varied beyond comparison; Shakespeare's every resource is drawn upon, his invention finds full scope. In *Coriolanus* it is disciplined, kept to its single channel, and the story moves lucidly and directly to its retributive end. And in one major difference most of the rest are rooted: in the part played in each by the idea of Rome. In each, of course, it is a vital part. Antony early forecasts his own ruin in that reckless

> Let Rome in Tiber melt, and the wide arch
> Of the ranged empire fall!

Cleopatra's first note of alarm lest she lose him sounds in the

> He was disposed to mirth; but on the sudden
> A Roman thought hath struck him.

and throughout she is a prey to her jealousy, hatred and dread of Rome. Still, this is little more than a background for the personal passion. But in *Coriolanus* everything centres upon Rome. It is the play's one sounding board. The springs of the action are there. Coriolanus himself sinks at last by comparison to something like second place. He returns for his revenge, and all thoughts and eyes are on him. He departs, self-defeated; and it is Volumnia who re-enters the city in triumph, hailed by a

> Behold our patroness, the life of Rome!

And his death thereafter in Corioles even approaches anticlimax.

But this fidelity to the larger, less personal theme lends the play a very Roman strength and solidity, which compensates to some degree, and in its kind, for the lack of such plenary inspiration as has given us Lear or Macbeth, colossal and then stripped to the soul. The play gains strength too from the keying of its action throughout to strife of one sort or another. Of no other of the plays can it be said that, but for an incidental scene or so, and for the stilled suspense in which we listen to Volumnia's ultimate pleadings, the quarrelling and fighting scarcely cease from beginning to end. It is dramatically the more important, then, that the opposing stresses should be kept fairly balanced, in sympathy as well as in force. Amid mere ebb and flow of violence the interest of the action could not be sustained. But the balance is adjusted and continually readjusted, the tension never quite relaxed. And the skill of the play's workmanship shows largely in this.

The story allows for scene after scene of actual fighting, and Shakespeare contrives for these every sort of variety: ranging in the war with the Volscians from the amazing sight of Marcius pitted against a whole city-full to the duel with Aufidius; in the struggle with the citizens from the victory where, sword in hand, he leads a handful of his friends against the rabble, a victory he is persuaded not to pursue, to the defeat in which this same rabble, better disciplined by the Tribunes, combine to banish him. And in the play's closing passages, the happy shouts of the Romans, freed from their fears, are contrasted with the spurious triumph of the Volscians.

The balance of sympathy also is fairly adjusted, neither side capturing—and keeping—overmuch. Shakespeare has been freely charged, in an age apt to be prejudiced in its favour, with bias against the populace. Allow for a little harmless ridicule and it is really not so. They are no match for Menenius in a contest of wit—although one of them, to his surprise, gamely stands up to him—

but they see through Marcius' mockery, for all that they are too polite to tell him so. In that scene of the 'garment of humility', indeed, his manners contrast most unfavourably with theirs. Individually, they seem simple, kindly creatures; collectively, they are doubtless unwise and unstable. They are human. Marcius has been their enemy, and they do not forget it. He declares that he remains so, and when he attacks them, they retaliate. They follow their leaders blindly, are misled and turn on them savagely at last. It is not a very sentimental survey, certainly. But why should it be?

The Tribunes are left the unqualified 'villains of the piece'; a surface of comic colouring—which by making them amusingly contemptible may make them a little less detestable—is the only mitigation allowed them. But not one of the characters with a capital share in the mêlée of the action is very sympathetically drawn. Not, certainly,

> Worthy Menenius Agrippa; one that hath always loved the people.

—so acclaimed by them at our first sight of him, but in fact, as we soon find, cajoling them and sneering at them by turns. Not Aufidius, unstable in good and ill. The untender Volumnia remains so to the last, heedless in her triumph of the price her son must pay for it; a point made implicitly only, but clearly enough to leave us feeling cold towards her. And Shakespeare treats Caius Marcius himself detachedly, as a judge might, without creative warmth. Both sides of his case are to be heard; and we see him first at his worst (an unusual introduction for a titular hero), bullying the hungry citizens. The balance is soon adjusted by evidence—the fighter seen actually fighting—that his valour exceeds all tales of it; in battle and after it he stands out as hero supreme. And his trial of character, when this begins, is lifted, at its crisis, to high ground. It is not his ill-conditioned egoism but his fervent championship of an unpopular faith that gets him driven from Rome. The balance shifts violently when he seeks recreant revenge for this, to be shifted again when at the last moment he abandons it and pays the penalty. Finally, something like justice is done.

The play's range of characters is not a wide one, for it is kept closely relevant to the demands of the action, and these do not by much overspread the direct channel of the story. But within this range Shakespeare works with complete surety. We have that most leisurely of openings, the tale of the Belly and the Members, and Marcius' first attack on the citizens—much of a distractingly different sort having to happen before that full quarrel is joined—is given good scope. The geography of the battle-scenes by Corioles is schemed for us as concisely as clearly. But we have their action at length; for this serves to fill out the characters of Marcius, of Cominius and Titus Lartius too, each the more himself by contrast with the others; the prudent Consul and the old warrior, so young at heart, who will

> lean upon one crutch and fight with t'other,
> Ere stay behind this business.

generously happy, both of them, in their arrogant young hero's glory. The dispute that leads to the banishment is thrashed out at fullest length, argued back and forth, and yet again, nothing significant left uncanvassed. Later, in the scene at Antium, which brings us the renegade Coriolanus, we note that Shakespeare gives as much space to the sly, flunkey commentings of Aufidius' servants upon the amazing business and their master's romantic aberration as he has to the encounter itself. This, besides lowering the tension, helps resolve the new combination into the unheroic key in which it will be worked out.

Shakespeare has now come to ask for more sheer acting from his actors than he did, for more meaning and feeling to be compressed occasionally into half a dozen words than would once have flowed from a rhetorical hundred, for expressive listening as well as expressive speech, for silence itself sometimes to be made eloquent.

> *Holds her by the hand, silent.*

—the play's most tragic moment, in which Marcius accepts defeat and in the sequel death at his mother's hand, confided to a simple stage direction.[2] Throughout the play action and words are expressively keyed together, the action of as great an import as the words. Marcius' share in the scene of the wearing of the gown of humility is as much picturing as speaking; and the mere sight of him later in his Roman dress, surrounded by the Volsces in theirs, sitting in council with them, marching into Corioles at their head—the graphic discord vivifies the play's ending.[3] The sight of the silently approaching figures of Volumnia, Virgilia and Valeria makes double effect; directly upon us, and upon us again through the effect made upon Marcius. And little though Virgilia says (and Valeria not a word), Volumnia so insistently joins them to her plea that their simple presence has an all but articulate value; while the actual spectacle of Marcius fighting singlehanded 'within Corioles gates' is better witness to his prowess than any of the 'acclamations hyperbolical' which he somewhat self-consciously decries. The memory of it, moreover, will not fade, only lie dormant until at the last it is rekindled by the magnificently trenchant

> 'Boy'! false hound!
> If you have writ your annals true, 'tis there,
> That, like an eagle in a dove-cote, I
> Fluttered your Volscians in Corioles:
> Alone I did it.

Here, then, we have a play of action dealing with men of action; and in none that Shakespeare wrote do action and character better supplement and balance each other.

The Characters

CAIUS MARCIUS

MARCIUS is by no means a sympathetic character, and Shakespeare's attitude towards him seems, as we say, to be less that of a creator than a judge. There is a sense in which—brought to it by the art of dramatist and actor—we can come to 'sympathize' even with the murderer Macbeth, as we can pity the murderer Othello, having learned to put ourselves imaginatively in their place. But we are left detached observers of Coriolanus; now admiring his valour, now exasperated by his harsh folly, touched occasionally by the flashes of nobility, the moments of gentleness. Yet we are never wholly at one with him, never made free of the inward man. And the juncture which could best bring this into play, the spiritual crisis in which he decides for his renegade revenge on Rome, is boldly and neatly sidestepped. It is strange, says Marcius in that one short soliloquy, how quickly enemies may become friends and friends turn enemies.

> So with me:
> My birth-place hate I, and my love's upon
> This enemy town.

We are (this is to tell us) past the play's turning point already. The crucial change in the man has already taken place; and of the process of it we learn nothing. But this is not necessarily a shortcoming on Shakespeare's part—as were Marcius a Hamlet it would be. *Was* there any such explicable process? He is not a man of reason, but of convictions and passionate impulses, which can land him in a sudden decision—and he will not know how he came by it. That may help make him a good fighter, less good, probably, as a general, certainly a poor politician. And it justifies Shakespeare's treatment of him here. By his mere looks, in the bitter humility— the old pride so quickly breaking through, as the unlucky Third Servingman discovers—with which he encourages Aufidius' servants to mock him, we are to discern the sufferings of his lonely exile, and surmise the pent-up wrath, vented at last in that blind resolve to be revenged on his own ungrateful people or let the Volsces take revenge on him. Shall we now, on such evidence, sufficiently surmise all this? That the thing, when it did happen, will have happened in a flash; we have seen amply enough of him by now to believe so. Critics have combed the text for some sign of the actual moment of its happening; since surely, they argue, Shakespeare could not have let such a significant one slip by unmarked; and one has been found hidden in an exclamatory 'O, the gods!' wrung from him at the very time of his banishing when he is taking leave of his mother and his wife. But this will not do. Tell the actor concerned that he is expected to convey to his audience in those three detached and unacknowledged words a sudden resolve to be revenged on the ungrateful city, and he will reasonably reply that it cannot be done. And while the maturer Shakespeare may certainly present his actors now and then with all but insuperable difficulties—creative imagination beckoning the interpreter towards very steep places indeed—never does he ask of them the impossible. What he does in this instance by a mere stroke of omission may seem to the *reader* of the play only to leave a rent in the texture of story and character. But in effect, and to the *spectator*, it is not so. Marcius could not appropriately be made to argue himself into such treason, as a Hamlet might, or discover the seeds of it in his nature, as might Macbeth. But picture and action significantly 'placed' are as legitimate and often as important a dramatic resource as the spoken word can be. And what, at this juncture, could be more fittingly eloquent than the simple sight—and the shock it must give us—of this haggard, hardly recognizable figure? It will flash into our imaginations, as words might not, a sense of the suffering that has brought him to such a pass.

Shakespeare does not shirk the less tolerable aspects of the character. Indeed he stresses them, since he first shows us the man at his worst—strange treatment for a hero!—and in the theatre first impressions cut deep. After the long and exceptionally leisurely opening of the tale of the Belly and the Members comes Marcius, like a tornado, bullying and abusing the hungry citizens; and while what he says of them may be true, it is no satisfying answer to their empty stomachs. But if this is the worst side of him the best side of that is turned to us a minute later, and within a few more the various contending forces of this most contentious of plays have been deployed, their differences established, Marcius in the centre of them.

Word comes that the Volsces are in arms, threatening Rome. He turns happily to welcome the news, and the war itself, which he has shrewdly foreseen. It will help 'vent our musty superfluity'; here is something quite other than the complaint that has driven the despised citizens (who listen in glum silence) to mutiny. To 'our best elders', the Consul Cominius and the Senators, who now appear, he is all disciplined deference, accepting, though, besides, their tributes paid to him as if these were his right, nor forgetting as he goes to fling a parting sneer at the 'worshipful mutiners'.

The new-made Tribunes, Brutus and Sicinius, have been listening in silence too; and now we have their comments on him, as unfriendly, truly, as his own conduct to the people they are to stand for has been unfair—unfair to the best in his nature, but an undeniable part of that truth about him which the play is so judicially to unfold. Proud, disdainful, insolent; the three notes are hit hard. The Tribunes attach to him by implication besides—as such men are apt to—some of their own politician's cunning. But in this, it will soon be made plain, they mistake him. Better for him had he had that sort of weapon with which to fight them.

The battle-scenes bring his most trenchant qualities into play. The amazing spectacle of his singlehanded fight 'within Corioles gates' is to be matched by his duel with Aufidius in which he takes on 'certain Volsces' too who come to their leader's aid, *till they be driven in breathless*, later by his stand against his fellow Romans, drawing his sword with a 'No; I'll die here', and contrasted with the yet later sight of him, truly alone, *in mean apparel, disguised and muffled*. Throughout the battle he is in his glory, and at his happiest, outshining and out-topping all the rest; hero indeed. But the more portraying strokes are not neglected. When his troops fall back he abuses them as roundly as he did the citizens; still this is in the stress of the fighting. When he calls inspiringly for volunteers to follow him in a desperate venture—

> If any such be here,
> As it were sin to doubt, that love this painting
> Wherein you see me smeared; if any fear
> Lesser his person than an ill report;
> If any think brave death outweighs bad life,
> And that his country's dearer than himself . . .

—these surly cowards of such a short while since, now *all shout and wave their swords; take him up in their arms, and cast up their caps.*[4] Marcius could win men if he would, it is plain, had he but a tithe of the confidence in them that he has in himself. Nor is it that he is mere cold-hearted egoist. At the very instant of victory he can remember the 'poor man', a prisoner, who once used him kindly, even as later, in the midst of his triumph he can think of the widows left in Corioles and the 'mothers that lack sons'. He shows contempt for the spoils of war, honest distaste for the praises his prowess wins him, and under their lavishing an all but boyish self-consciousness.

This last trait (of Shakespeare's own importing: it has no place in Plutarch) is turned to varying account throughout the play. In the boyishness, the reckless high spirits with which he flings himself into battle, there is saving grace; even the thrasonical bragging to Aufidius before they fight is purged of offence if it comes as their mere overflow.[5] The question is not one of years. Marcius' actual age is not determined, and in North is only implied by the fact that he first went to the wars 'being but a strippling', and that when he stands for Consul he has seen seventeen years' service. He might then, by this, be about thirty-two, and as mature a man as the maturer Hamlet. But more than one thing in the story gives colour to youthfulness of temper. His boyish prowess, repeatedly stressed, suggests it; so do his rash decisions; so does his continued deference to his mother. And Shakespeare takes and enlarges on this means of mitigating the harshness which makes him—as North has it—so 'churlish, uncivill and altogether unfit for any man's conversation', to touch him with an unruly charm instead.

It is in the self-consciousness that the flaw lies. His repeated protests against the praises lavished on him become somewhat less then genuine. During the traffic of the battle, to generous old Titus Lartius:

> Sir, praise me not;
> My work hath yet not warmed me. . . .

And again:

> Pray now, no more: my mother,
> Who has a charter to extol her blood,
> When she does praise me, grieves me. . . .

And yet again, in protest to his general, not very graciously:

> You shout me forth
> In acclamations hyperbolical;
> As if I loved my little should be dieted
> In praises sauced with lies.

—this is not modesty (as Cominius kindly calls it), rather an inverted pride. Neglect to praise him; he will be the first to resent that!

We are shown one aspect after another of this obsessing self-consciousness. He will not even make himself sit still and listen respectfully to the Senate's official tribute to him, but must be up and away in the middle of it with a

> I had rather have one scratch my head i' the sun
> When the alarum were struck than idly sit
> To hear my nothings monstered.

His desperate discomfort standing in the market place in the gown of humility is positively comic.

> May I change these garments?

—his first request when the ordeal is over. He pictures himself with dramatic clarity returning there shamefaced to ask pardon of the despised citizens; he cannot resist, even at this critical moment, the false modesty of

> Scratches with briers;
> Scars to move laughter only.

when his friends once more be-laud his 'war-like service' and cite his many wounds. Later, he is most conscious of the effect he is making in his picturesque disgrace upon Aufidius and the lackeys. Lastly, he provokes his own death by losing all control under the petty insult of Aufidius' 'Boy!'

Yet such self-consciousness is not self-knowledge. Possessing but a spice of *this*, would he ever have taken his rash, revengeful vow to destroy Rome?—which, put to the ultimate test, proves no more stable than does Aufidius' febrile conversion to his cause. At the critical moment he stands firm against Cominius, certainly. But with Menenius—though he dismissed him harshly—he has afterwards to own that, under guise of firmness, he *has* yielded, even if it be only 'a very little'. And the mere news of the coming of his wife and mother seems to paralyze him:

> Shall I be tempted to infringe my vow
> In the same time 'tis made? I will not.

—the desperate 'I will not' telling us plainly that in his heart he knows already that he will. He is no true renegade. Striving to be false to Rome, he is false to himself.

And this his instinct—his unclouded, unselfconscious self-knowledge—has warned him more than once that he cannot afford to be. He was so—if harmlessly; for it was a trivial matter, and Shakespeare stresses the comic aspect of it—when after swearing he never would he *did* put on the gown of humility. He is about to be again, and in a matter of more consequence, when, under protest—

> Would you have me
> False to my nature? Rather say I play
> The man I am.

—he is letting Volumnia persuade him to recant before the people the faith he has just so ardently professed to them. But he finds when he tries to that he cannot. And it is in the violent recoil from this attempt to be other than he is that he strikes his most genuinely heroic note, with the ineffably proud retort to his sentence of banishment, the 'I banish you.'

Wrong-headed, intolerant and intolerable in his dealings with the citizens he may be, but upon the actual issues between them is he so wrong? He foresaw the first Volscian attack when the Senators—'our best elders'—did not, and the hungry populace could think of nothing but their hunger. Victory won and a 'good' peace granted the enemy (a little to his impatience), himself made Consul, he foresees another attack—

> So then the Volsces stand but as at first,
> Ready, when time shall prompt them, to make road
> Upon's again.

—not imagining, however, who, in the amazing irony of events, will lead it! He has foreseen, besides, from the beginning, that the new-made Tribunate

> will in time
> Win upon power, and throw forth greater themes
> For insurrections arguing.

And who is to say that he is wrong in his protest against the 'popular shall . . . the greater poll . . . the yea and no of general ignorance' being let outweigh experienced wisdom. What answer is there to his passionate

> my soul aches
> To know, when two authorities are up,
> Neither supreme, how soon confusion
> May enter, 'twixt the gap of both and take
> The one by the other.

Wrong or right, however, he must abide by his own convictions: honestly he can no other. He foresaw that too from the beginning, when Volumnia first held him out hopes of the consulate and he told her:

> Know, good mother,
> I had rather be their servant in my way
> Than sway with them in theirs.

For a man can do no better than be himself at his best. Sometimes it may even strangely seem that his quality lies rather in the worse than the better part of him; then we must take the rough with the smooth.

Play and character become truly tragic only when Marcius, to be traitor to Rome, must turn traitor to himself. The actual turning, as we said, we do not see, we are shown the thing already inwardly done. And the tragedy is uncovered in something like a reversal of the process, in the tragic failure to undo the thing once done, once begun even. It is ironic tragedy, too. Marcius has been used to meet fortune, good or bad, in the open. But from that dark moment in Antium, of the bitter

> My birth-place hate I, and my love's upon
> This enemy town.

everything with him and within him turns to mockery. Aufidius' extravagant homage to him will soon show itself a cheat. It is a false façade of him seeming to sit there

> in gold, his eye
> Red as 'twould burn Rome . . .

And when he has finally yielded to his mother's prayers he looks up to find that

> the heavens do ope,
> The gods look down, and this unnatural scene
> They laugh at.

He could go back to Rome—the 'clusters who did hoot him out o' the city' now as ready to 'roar him in again'—thanked for his weakness and kindness, and forgiven—he Coriolanus forgiven! But nor is that his nature. He is at least no weathercock. He has turned against the Romans, he will stay loyal now to the Volsces.[6]

Mockery piles on mockery in Corioles. The people there are something the same problem that they were in Rome. Aufidius, with his great repute, has still to observe their temper. And of Coriolanus, even of him, it can be said that he

> Intends to appear before the people, hoping
> To purge himself with words . . .

And—though first, truly, to the lords of the city—so, *the Commoners being with him*, he does, boasting of the spoils and the

> full third part
> The charges of the action . . .

he has brought back. When till now did he value such pinchbeck glory? In Rome he was plunged from triumph into obloquy. Now it is the fickle commoners of Corioles that turn on him, cheering him back at one moment, tearing him to pieces the next. When last these same Volsces swarmed round him he was one against all of them, and victor. They make better business of it now.

Coriolanus, then, is a character not inwardly evolved, as the greater tragic characters are, but seen from without. Seen and moulded, however, in the round; and as consistent and solid a figure as Shakespeare ever put in motion.

VOLUMNIA

The relations between mother and son and the likeness and difference between them are at the core of the play. The likeness is patent. It is she, he is wont to say, whose praise first made him a soldier. She rejoices in his prowess, gleefully in his very wounds, has the tale of them by heart, could dance for joy at his return for the third time with the oaken garland, wounded yet again. If martial spirit were all she would seem to be almost more soldier than he. And when the fateful struggle between them comes it is the grimmer for this.

As a woman she has no overt part in the political quarrel with the Tribunes; and, in that phase of the action, it is not until, amid the violence of its crisis, Marcius seeks a breathing-space in his house and hers, that we see or hear from her at all. But then she astonishes us—and him. For until now she has seemed as stiff, and stiffer than he, in pride. As to the Tribunes and their kind, she has ignored them, but had been wont, he says,

> To call them woollen vessels, things created
> To buy and sell with groats, to show bare heads
> In congregations, to yawn, be still and wonder
> When one but of my ordinance stood up
> To speak of peace or war . . .

Yet now, when trouble comes, from unashamed policy she would have him humble himself to them, recant his word and cheat them even in recanting, 'mountebank their loves'. He is to be, he protests, false to his nature; and she is setting him an example by being false to hers. She persuades him to it: yet fruitlessly since, tested, his nature rebels. It will take more than this: defeat and banishment and, later, suffering and blind anger, to trap him into swearing that oath of unnatural vengeance which it will prove beyond his power to keep. She will set out again to persuade him to break it, and, spending her last ounce of strength and influence, she will succeed. And then it will bear fruit; salvation for Rome, but, for him, bitter fruit indeed.

In a central scene, then, and at one of the play's chief turning points, we have this truly unexpected exhibition of difference between the two. Wilful and stubborn he may be, but, to his credit, he is not the mere overgrown spoiled child which the extravagance of her praise might so easily have made him. He turns from praise with the touch of affectation we have noted; from hers the more genuinely, remembering how much he once owed to it. But in his quarrel with the Tribunes he stands fearlessly for a cause. This is enshrined in egoism doubtless, but is not, he proudly feels, the poorer for that; since he stands, in what he has done and is, for what is best in Rome and he will never shrink from proclaiming it and his faith in it, no matter the moment's consequence. Volumnia, astonishingly the opposite, shows herself at once shrewdly critical, worldly-wise—

O, sir, sir, sir,
I would have had you put your power well on
Before you had worn it out.

—and shrewder yet:

You might have been enough the man you are
With striving less to be so. . . .

with irony to follow for the deflating of his anger, and
the cold realism of

I have a heart as little apt as yours,
But yet a brain that leads my use of anger
To better vantage.

—a calculated use of it. And it will no more dishonour
him (she easily argues) to manoeuvre a crooked way back
into his fellow countrymen's favour than it would in
wartime to

take in a town with gentle words.

She herself, here and now, lavishes the gentlest on him;
these failing, tries her 'use of anger', pretended or real,
with a

At thy choice, then:
To beg of thee it is my more dishonour
Than thou of them. Come all to ruin. . . .
Do your will.

He is the cause she stands for—that is the truth; and
that he will not help her, and himself, by unscrupulously
putting it before all other, exasperates her. He pays in
banishment the penalty of his scruples. She is passion-
ately for him in defeat as in victory, and but the more
enraged with his enemies for their profiting by his
high-minded unwisdom. After this, again, she is absent

from the action for many scenes; and again, re-entering it, she sounds an unexpected note.

Mark now the dramatic strategy, as Shakespeare plans it, of her share in the women's appeal to Marcius for mercy upon Rome. Simply the sight of her and of his wife and son stirs him. She does not speak at first; only

>   My mother bows,
>   As if Olympus to a molehill should
>   In supplication nod. . . .

The constricted figure has an eloquence of its own. His wife, softly reproachful, wins the first response from him. Not until he kneels does Volumnia speak, outdoing him then by herself kneeling, a shade of irony—no more!—in the ostentation of her gesture. After which, as with a certain confidence in this their meeting again, the plea is launched. She can be eloquent now, as never before. It is an eloquence inspired by that clarity of vision which imminent tragedy brings:

>   for how can we,
>   Alas! how can we for our country pray,
>   Whereto we are bound, together with thy victory,
>   Whereto we are bound? Alack! or we must lose
>   The country, our dear nurse, or else thy person,
>   Our comfort in the country. We must find
>   An evident calamity, though we had
>   Our wish, which side should win; for either thou
>   Must, as a foreign recreant, be led
>   With manacles through our streets, or else
>   Triumphantly tread on thy country's ruin,
>   And bear the palm for having bravely shed
>   Thy wife and children's blood.

The new note follows; a new note indeed:

> If it were so that our request did tend
> To save the Romans, thereby to destroy
> The Volsces whom you serve, you might condemn us
> As poisonous of your honour: no; our suit
> Is that you reconcile them: while the Volsces
> May say 'This mercy we have showed'; the Romans,
> 'This we received'; and each in either side
> Give the all-hail to thee, and cry 'Be blest
> For making up this peace!'

If he 'mused' before at her indifference to his heroic stand against the mob for his proud conscience' sake, what will his retort be now to this talk of peace—of peace for its own sake; to such a warning from her as

> Thou knowest, great son,
> The end of war's uncertain. . . .

to her disparaging

> Thou hast affected the fine strains of honour. . . .

her

> Think'st thou it honourable for a noble man
> Still to remember wrongs?

It has taken truly a terrible revolution to bring her to this: no less than the sight of her son, his country's hero, turned his country's enemy, her own son, her enemy. And she begins to feel nevertheless that she is beaten, that her high arguments are breaking against his stubborn silence. Yet she is as tenacious a fighter in her way as ever we have found him to be, and she flings herself and the forces with her—mother, wife, child, the whole womanhood of Rome—desperately into the struggle:

> Daughter, speak you:
> He cares not for your weeping. Speak thou, boy:

> Perhaps thy childishness will move him more
> Than can our reasons.

Their silence had begun it, as they stood ranged accusingly before him; by some means they must break his silence now. Volumnia chides and clamours:

> There's no man in the world
> More bound to's mother; yet here he lets me prate
> Like one i' the stocks. Thou has never in thy life
> Shewed thy dear mother any courtesy....

By whatever means let her win! But she can fight a losing battle as fiercely as he could a winning one:

> Down, ladies; let us shame him with our knees.

Then with a Parthian scorn:

> Come, let us go:
> This fellow had a Volscian to his mother:
> His wife is in Corioles, and his child
> Like him by chance.

Yet she has won. Throwing her strength in to the very last, even at the admitted moment of defeat—

> Yet give us our despatch:
> I am husht until our city be a-fire,
> And then I'll speak a little.

—she had already won.

The very moment during his tenacious silence when his will yielded has been covered by silence too. And now she does not answer his low, searching

> O, mother, mother!
> What have you done?

when it emerges from the silence, nor respond at all to the unequivocal

> O, my mother, mother! O!
> You have won a happy victory to Rome;
> But for your son, believe it, O, believe it,
> Most dangerously you have with him prevailed,
> If not most mortal to him.

So possessed by her victory, is she, as to be incapable of a second thought? Is she so spent with the strain of her pleading that she faces Rome again a little later, and its frenzied welcome, in a very daze? Marcius, in any case, as with a new-learned magnanimity, shepherds away more talk of his defeat, thoughts of his fate. And her part in the play is done.[7]

It ends, as does her son's—as may be said of the whole play—amid the ironic laughter of the gods; she is unaware, that is all, of the successive mockeries in the event, made at last so bitterly plain to him. She has bred him to be at once Rome's hero and Rome's enemy. She has begged Rome's life of him, and, in winning it, is obviously sending him to his death. And we last see her welcomed triumphantly back to Rome even as he once was, flowers strewed before her, amid cries of

> Unshout the noise that banished Marcius;
> Repeal him with the welcome of his mother. . . .

But it is too late for that. And tragedy of character does not work out in such happy confusions of popular acclaim.

It is a chill parting, this with Volumnia; our last sight of her—nothing nearer—parading through Rome, her back turned upon Marcius himself and the essential tragedy's imminent consummation.

AUFIDIUS

It takes all Shakespeare's skill to make Aufidius fully effective within the space which the planning of the action allows him—and perhaps he does not wholly succeed. For a while it is not so difficult. He is admitted on all hands to be Marcius' rival and to come short of him by little. Marcius' first word of him is that

> I sin in envying his nobility,
> And were I anything but what I am,
> I would wish me only he.

He is secondary hero. And when within a moment or so we see the man himself he is telling the Senators of Corioles:

> If we and Caius Marcius chance to meet,
> 'Tis sworn between us we shall ever strike
> Till one can do no more.

Volumnia, imagining glorious things, can see her Marcius

> pluck Aufidius down by the hair . . .

In the battle the Corioles taunt the Romans with

> There is Aufidius: list, what work he makes
> Amongst your cloven army.

while to Marcius, whether far off—

> There is the man of my soul's hate, Aufidius. . . .

—or within reach—

> Set me against Aufidius and his Antiats. . . .

—he is an obsession. And when they do meet and fight, Aufidius, if bettered, is not beaten. To this point, then, however little we may see of him, he is brought to our minds in each succeeding scene, and is emphatically lodged there when he is so unconsentingly rescued in the duel with his famous enemy by 'certain

Volsces' (anonymous: common soldiers presumably, therefore):

> Officious, and not valiant, you have shamed me
> In your condemned seconds.

And, since we shall not see him thereafter for some time,
this note of shame, and of the crooked passion it can
rouse in the man, is enlarged and given what will be
memorable place in a scene coming but a little later.

> Five times, Marcius,
> I have fought with thee; so often hast thou beat me,
> And wouldst do so, I think, should we encounter
> As often as we eat.[8]

Frank confession! But now

> mine   emulation
> Hath not that honour in't it had; for where
> I thought to crush him in an equal force,
> True sword to sword, I'll potch at him some way
> Or wrath or craft may get him. . . .
> Where I find him, were it
> At home, upon my brother's guard, even there,
> Against the hospitable canon, would I
> Wash my fierce hands in's heart.

We shall certainly recall that—and be given good cause
to—when, all amazingly, the event so falls out. The
scheme of the action allows Aufidius very limited space;
but we have thus far been kept conscious of him
throughout. From now, even until he emerges into it
again, he does not go quite without mention, and we
shall have lodged in mind what he may mean to it when
he does. It is able stagecraft.

In a cruder play Aufidius and the Volsces might be
made to serve as 'villains of the piece'. But Shakespeare

is not painting in such ultra-patriotic black and white.
We are on the Roman side, and they are 'foreigners'; so
their worse, not their better, aspect is naturally turned
towards us. The victorious Romans give them a 'good'
peace, Titus Lartius being commanded to send back
from their captured city

> to Rome
> The best, with whom we may articulate,
> For their own good and ours.

They, when their victorious turn comes, so we hear,

> looked
> For no less spoil than glory . . .

Shakespeare shades them somewhat. But the balance is
not unfairly held.

Aufidius, then, re-enters the action at its most critical
juncture, and to play for the moment a surprising part
in it. Here, in this wine-flushed host to the nobles of
Antium, is quite another man; and not only in the look
of him but, yet more surprisingly—suspense resolved—in
the deep-sworn enemy turned ecstatic comrade. From
that

> Nor sleep, nor sanctuary,
> Being naked, sick, nor fane nor Capitol,
> The prayers of priests, nor times of sacrifice,
> Embarquements all of fury, shall lift up
> Their rotten privilege and custom 'gainst
> My hate to Marcius.

we are at a glowing

> Let me twine
> Mine arms about that body, where against
> My grained ash an hundred times hath broke

And scarred the moon with splinters: here I clip
The anvil of my sword, and do contest
As hotly and as nobly with thy love
As ever in ambitious strength I did
Contend against thy valour.

It is a turning point indeed, and doubly so; the revolution in Marcius is barely set forth before it is matched with this. The two revolutions differ as the two men do; the one a plunging through defeat and misery from confident pride to obdurate bitterness; that in Aufidius a sudden emotional overthrow, sprung by this startling proffer, this attack upon a weakness in him which he would never think to defend. Yet there is a likeness between them too. And they are in keeping, both, with the rest of the play, its extremes of passion and their instabilities; the weather-cock-swaying of the citizens, Volumnia's violence and arbitrary shifts. Marcius himself we shall see will be unable to abide by his treason to the end; and Aufidius, we shall very quickly guess, will not long sustain this unnatural change. Recurring ironies fitting into the scheme of tragic irony which informs the whole action.

This 'strange alteration'—reflected too in the freakish comment of the servants—gives us a fresh, and, for the moment, an alert interest in Aufidius. From now to the end the stagecraft actuating him remains as able; and if here and there the figure seems to lack vitality, to be a little word-locked, why, livelier development of this new aspect of the man might well make more demands on the play's space than could be spared, or such a turn of inspiration as Shakespeare (even he!) has not unquestionably at command. But he does not dodge nor skip a step in the completing of the character. And, within a scene or so, to begin this, we see Aufidius again—quite disillusioned.

Thinking better of things is a dry business; and this ancillary scene, shared with an anonymous Lieutenant, will appropriately be none of the liveliest. But the matter of it is a strengthening rivet in the character scheme of the play. Aufidius' sobered reaction from his rhapsodies to the coldest common sense—hints dropped moreover of revengeful traps already laid for Marcius; Aufidius to be revenged on him for his own access of too generous folly, the hardest thing forgivable—this will redress any balance of sympathy lost between the two for the action's last phase. We have no violent swing back to the fanatically sportsmanlike hatred with which they started. On the contrary, to Aufidius is given in the scene's last speech the most measured and balanced of summarizings of his rival's qualities and failings. And for Marcius it is in this quiet reasonable accounting that his worst danger can be foreseen. Mastery in soldiership—who has ever denied him that? He has not even to exercise it now:

> All places yield to him ere he sits down;
> And . . .

—despite his treason; because of it indeed—

> the nobility of Rome are his:
> The Senators and Patricians love him too. . . .
> I think he'll be to Rome
> As is the asprey to the fish, who takes it
> By sovereignty of nature. . . .

Aufidius, lacking just that sovereignty, could not look his own problem more fairly in the face. For, indeed, he had better know just where he has the worse of it, that being the second-rate man's due approach to getting the better of it after all. He may next encourage himself by listing—though with every scruple and reserve—Marcius' failings too: pride, temper, intolerance and the rest, and by recognizing that in this discordant world men have the defects of their qualities and the qualities of their defects; and that at best, what is more,

> our virtues
> Lie in the interpretation of the time. . . .

—which may prove for us or against us; and whichever way

> One fire drives out one fire; one nail, one nail;
> Rights by rights founder, strengths by strengths do fail.

Fortune, with a little patient aid, is ever ready to turn her wheel:

> When, Caius, Rome is thine
> Thou art poor'st of all; then shortly art thou mine.

Both speech and scene demand of their audience close attention, closer, perhaps, than such detached argument will currently command at this juncture in a play unless it be embodied in some central, radiating figure. It is the more notable that Shakespeare should here, so to speak, be forcing his meaning through the recalcitrant lines.[9] But his aim, it would seem, is to give a rational substance to the figure, of such a sort as will keep us an Aufidius expressively if cryptically observant through succeeding scenes while we await the due restoring of the natural open enmity between the two.

It comes with relief.

> How is it with our general?

his fellow conspirators ask.

> Even so
> As with a man by his own alms empoisoned,
> And with his charity slain.

But he is free now of his false position and on his own ground again, and the ills done him are glib upon his tongue. He must be cautiously in the right at all points:

> And my pretext to strike at him admits
> A good construction. I raised him, and I pawned
> Mine honour for his truth. . . .

More than so, he

> took some pride
> To do myself this wrong . . .

—he is fuelling up with virtuous indignation, until, at the touch of a match, Coriolanus himself can be trusted to fire out in fury, no moral excuses needed. 'Traitor . . . unholy braggart . . . boy of tears . . . boy!'—it is the last spark that sets all ablaze.

Aufidius' philosophic mind has not endured; nor does the one-time gallantry. 'My valour's poisoned . . . '—we are back at that. He is no coward, we know; has ever been ready to fight. It is only that, now or never, he must have the best of it, and he has made all sure. So, duly provoked

> *The Conspirators draw, and kill Coriolanus, who falls. . . .*

Upon which, though, he cannot resist it:

> *Aufidius stands on him.*[10]

Shakespeare, in the maturity of his skill, knows how to give as much meaning to a significantly placed gesture as to a speech or more. There are two gestures here, the insolent treading of the slain man under foot, with the quick attempt in face of the shocked outcry to excuse it:

My noble masters, hear me speak.

then the response to the reproach:

> O, Tullus!
> Thou hast done a deed whereat valour will weep.
> Tread not upon him. Masters . . .

which can but be its shamed and embarrassed lifting, the more eloquent of Aufidius, this. The more fittingly unheroic, besides, the ending. The lords of the city have been honourable enemies.

> Peace, ho! no outrage: peace!
> The man is noble and his fame folds in
> This orb o' the earth. His last offences to us
> Shall have judicious hearing.

The sight of the outrage done him horrifies them. But as Aufidius promptly argues,

> My lords, when you shall know, as in this rage
> Provoked by him, you cannot, the great danger
> Which this man's life did owe you, you'll rejoice
> That he is thus cut off.

and, truly, as they'll in fairness soon admit:

> His own impatience
> Takes from Aufidius a great part of blame. . . .

Common sense supervenes:

> Let's make the best of it.

And Aufidius can say with truth, the man being safely dead:

> My rage is gone,
> And I am struck with sorrow.

MENENIUS

Menenius makes one in the ironically figured pattern of character. He is set outwardly—and at the play's very start—in sharp contrast to Coriolanus himself:

> Worthy Menenius Agrippa; one that hath always loved the people.

—so even the disgruntled citizens admit. Jovial, humorous, reasonable; what could be less like the intolerant, rough-tongued young soldier, whose pride it is that

> He would not flatter Neptune for his trident,
> Or Jove for's power to thunder.

But soon enough we notice that behind the cajoling

> Why, masters, my good friends, mine honest neighbours . . .

and the merry tale that sets them laughing—at each other it is, too!—his complete indifference to their troubles. Marcius, storming, would have had

> the nobility lay aside their ruth,
> And let me use my sword.

Menenius has taken the cannier way; and here already, at no cost but fair words,

> these are almost thoroughly persuaded;
> For though abundantly they lack discretion,
> Yet are they passing cowardly.

Nor does he scruple, it would seem, to say so in their hearing.

Menenius is to pervade the play, yet as an auxiliary character only. This full and vivid shaping of the figure so early has one incidental advantage then; the lightest future touch—and however slight be its connection with the main action—will be effective. And in all the plays there are few livelier or more individual characters.

An old gentleman of 'character', an 'original', to his friends the best of friends; his fighting spirit has not flagged either with the years, and he fights the more cleverly with his tongue for his sole weapon, if the more spitefully now and then. Would Marcius but profit by it his counsel might steer him to safety. He loves him as a man his own son, delights in his prowess and fame. He knows him too, better than does Volumnia, and is quick to persuade him that, willy-nilly, he must don that vext 'gown of humility', sticks to him too till he has it on, shepherds him to the very verge of the actual ordeal, only quits him then with almost comic misgiving, to return at the first moment as proud as a nurse of a well-behaved child at a party.

The rioting in the market place tells on his age. While he stands loyally by Marcius he pleads breathlessly with each disputant in turn, flatters even the loathed Tribunes. But he never loses his head, nor his sense of humour either, gives a savingly comic twist to Marcius' militant

> On fair ground
> I could beat forty of them.

(as indeed we know and see) by his own merry

> I could myself
> Take up a brace of the best of them; yea, the two Tribunes.

Nor does he ignore his own side's failings. Of Marcius, momentarily relieved of his incendiary presence:

> His nature is too noble for the world . . .
>   What the vengeance!
> Could he not speak 'em fair?

—into which combination of tempers do these heroes drive us. But here he is at his best, with that frank

> As I do know the Consul's worthiness,
> So can I name his faults.

and in his plea for Rome's honour, threats of death and banishment overhanging the man who has so fought for her:

> Now the good gods forbid
> That our renowned Rome, whose gratitude
> Towards her deserved children is enrolled
> In Jove's own book, like an unnatural dam
> Should now eat up her own! . . .
> What has he done to Rome that's worthy death?
> Killing our enemies, the blood he hath lost
> Which, I dare vouch, is more than that he hath,
> By many an ounce—he dropped it for his country;
> And what is left, to lose it by his country,
> Were to us all, that do't and suffer it,
> A brand to the end o' the world.

—the artful old man with his crotchets turned to the grave patrician; the verse as fittingly strong and clear.

But to the last moment he is pliably for give-and-take, real or pretended, wailing to his self-wrecked hero a despairing

> Is this the promise that you made your mother?

and past the last moment staying faithfully by him, till he finds place in that sad journey to the gates.

> Thou old and true Menenius,
> Thy tears are salter than a younger man's,
> And venemous to thine eyes.

—yet more quickly dried to calm, it seems. (Here comes one of Shakespeare's incidental touches of veracity.) The fight finished and lost, the women—Volumnia, even Virgilia—pass from tears to anger, Menenius to all that is most pacific. There is no more to be done, and he is very, very weary; though if he

> could shake off but one seven years
> From these old arms and legs ...

he'd tramp it too by Marcius' side with the best. But Marcius gone, not even the sight of the swaggering Tribunes rouses him. Finally, for the distraught and shaken mother and wife he has nothing but a kindly

> Peace, peace! be not so loud.

unless it be, as Brutus and Sicinius sheer off, the consolation of

> You have told them home,
> And, by my troth, you have cause. . . .

with the yet solider comfort of

> You'll sup with me?

It is unheroic, doubtless, thus to finish such a day. But he is not heroic!

Tit for tat is hard to resist; nor, certainly, is Menenius a man to miss a chance of it when it comes. While Marcius is banished and the Tribunes are in power he keeps a stiff lip in opposition, foxing enough to warrant their sarcastic

> O! he is grown most kind
> Of late. Hail, sir!

But when the sudden, startling turn of fortune comes, tidings of Marcius' and Aufidius' dread approach, the old Menenius reappears, lively and ready as ever:

> What news? what news? . . .
> What's the news? what's the news? . . .
> Pray, now your news? . . .
> Pray, your news?

News suiting his ironic temper in defeat, of the prospect of his hero's sacking of his city; a pretty contradiction, however deserved. But here even Menenius' sense of irony will be stretched a little. He can turn, however, sarcastically on the Tribunes:

> You have made good work,
> You and your apron men. . . .
> You and your crafts! You have crafted fair!

If they shirk the blame, what can the answer to that be but

> How! was't we? . . .

But it was.

> We loved him; but, like beasts
> And cowardly nobles, gave way unto your clusters,
> Who did hoot him out o' the city.

And will mere words now win pardon for either lot of them? Menenius takes delight in assuring the wretched citizens—a troop of them arriving at this juncture—in assuring them under the crestfallen Tribunes' very noses that

> not a hair upon a soldier's head
> Which will not prove a whip: as many coxcombs
> As you threw caps up will he tumble down
> And pay you for your voices.

He once more finds himself, indeed, the old racily tongued Menenius of our first acquaintance, haranguing the biddable crowd. Brutus and Sicinius make a last effort to regain their followers' confidence, but with little enough left in themselves, it seems. The one-time winners throw in their hands, and the losers are left to make the best of a bad job between them.

Menenius does not fancy suffering himself the great man's treatment of Cominius. It was Cominius' business (who preceded him as Consul) to be the first to go begging forgiveness. Once

> He called me father:
> But what o' that? . . .
> Nay, if he coyed
> To hear Cominius speak, I'll keep at home.

But what he wants is to be pressed into going; and for that he flagrantly plays, until flattery in full measure sends the old man off, breezily confident that with him to do it the task is as good as done.

Menenius makes, dramatically speaking, a good end. He plays the statesman with the soldiers guarding Coriolanus, they, enjoyably, the soldier with him. He is 'an officer of state', and he and Rome, things at the worst, retain, one hopes, their dignity. But he's not the first to come (here the close-packing of the action, the tale of Cominius' attempt, adds to the effect of this); and

> our general
> Will no more hear from thence.

Then begins the tussle, familiar to any wartime, between soldier and civilian, the Somebody in peace and Nobody in war, whose condescending

> Good my friends,
> If you have heard your general talk of Rome,

> And of his friends there, it is lots to blanks,
> My name hath touched your ears: it's Menenius.

earns from a sentry under orders no more than a cool

> Be it so; go back: the virtue of your name
> Is not here passable.

Menenius adds to his credit one civilian virtue after
another:

> I tell thee, fellow,
> Thy general is my lover: I have been
> The book of his good acts, whence men have read
> His fame unparalleled, haply amplified:
> For I have ever verified my friends,
> Of whom he's chief. . . .

—and it is true!—

> with all the size that verity
> Would without lapsing suffer . . .

each as unavailingly as the last. Indignation does not
serve.

> Sirrah, if thy captain knew I were here, he would use me
> with estimation.
> Come, my captain knows you not.
> I mean thy general.
> My general cares not for you. Back, I say, go; lest I let
> forth your half-pint of blood. . . .

—the soldier's conclusive argument. Marcius' own appearance, with Aufidius in quiet partnership, puts the
matter to the proof.

Nowhere in the play do we find the pattern of its
character-planning more effectively turned and coloured.
The comic charged with emotion; what more human?

Old Menenius fatuously insisting upon the sentries discomfiting him, yet heartbroken in his pleading; and it is—we see it—with a cracked heart that Marcius repulses him, that harsh 'Away'! little better than a blow in the face. And he must accept Aufidius' praise for it, the dry

> You keep a constant temper.

The sentries allowed their mockery, if they fancy they can outmock this gallant old patrician in defeat they are vastly mistaken. He can still give back better than he gets:

> I neither care for the world, nor your general: for such things as you, I can scarce think there's any, y'are so slight....

Civilian though he be, he has a weapon of which they cannot rob him:

> He that hath a will to die by himself, fears it not from another. Let your general do his worst. For you, be that you are, long; and your misery increase with your age! [His does!] I say to you, as I was said to, Away!

—and he is gone; bearing off the honours with him, thinks one of these Volscians, duly impressed:

> A noble fellow, I warrant him.

the other of tougher mind:

> The worthy fellow is our general: he's the rock, the oak not to be wind-shaken.

The closely contrived action allows for yet one small turn more in the pattern of character, and typical—fully so—it shall be. The trembling Sicinius awaits tidings; not to be mitigated. But if Menenius has been beaten, let there be no belittling the battle lost; and, if *he* cannot come home winner, who may? Did not Cominius tell them how

The tartness of his face sours ripe grapes; when he walks
he moves like an engine, and the ground shrinks before his
treading. . . . He sits in his state, as a thing made for Alex-
ander. . . .

Sicinius may bleat that

> He loved his mother dearly.

Forlornest of hopes, retorted on by

> So did he me; and he no more remembers his mother
> now than an eight-year-old horse. . . . Mark what mercy his
> mother shall bring from him: there is no more mercy in him
> than there is milk in a male tiger. . . .

Menenius, be it remembered, does not know what has
passed since his plea was repulsed. For all that he does
know it is the right sort of medicine he is administer-
ing—having first swallowed it himself with that cheerful
courage, which it is lets him in turn so enjoy forcing it
down the unhappy Tribune's own throat. Once more
comes the solacing refrain:

> and all this is 'long of you.

with, for a closing chord, each striking his own note,
Sicinius' pitiful

> The gods be good unto us!

the old politician, gamer:

> No, in such a case the gods will not be good unto us.
> When we banished him we respected not them, and, he
> returning to break our necks, they respect not us.

Take the rough with the smooth and look facts in the
face; as wholesome a lesson in politics as lay in the tale

of the Belly and the Members. Whereupon, the concluding good news brought and confirmed, Menenius can
take this also as coolly—for all that he'll let the two
scurvy cowards of Tribunes discover! And with this he
is caught back into the ending central stream of the
play's action, lively to his last word.

THE TRIBUNES

Brutus and Sicinius make a listening and a not
promptly identifiable first appearance. The aristocrats,
assembled by the rumours of war, depart elated, the
humiliated citizens steal away, leaving these two—the
new Tribunes, will they be?—to savour their comments:

> Was ever man so proud as is this Marcius?
> He has no equal.

They are not of the simple calibre of their followers, that
is at once made plain; the craftiest of politicians, rather,
with Brutus to belittle—and slander—Marcius, true pol-
itician-wise:

> Fame, at the which he aims,
> In whom already he's well-graced, can not
> Better be held nor more attained than by
> A place below the first; for what miscarries
> Shall be the general's fault, though he perform
> To the utmost of a man; and giddy censure
> Will then cry out of Marcius, 'O, if he
> Had borne the business!'

Sicinius joining in. The twenty-five-line interchange of
cynical judgment stamps them vividly enough on our
memory: a binding-up of the story; for between now and
our next encounter with them the whole Volscian war
is to pass.

We find them again still in Rome (where they are is always Rome); of consequence now, evidently, among the people, but uneasily awaiting the hero's return, decrying him, fearing for their chances beside him. It is now that they take colour as comic villains; this thanks to Menenius, who finds ridicule, in which he is bluffly expert, the best weapon with which to torment them. One effect of this will be that while we, with the more sympathetic Menenius, may detest and make fun of them, in other bearings they are still the two sharp politicians. Shakespeare disposes his sides for the coming combat with great address. Here are these two, playing the game by its rules, yielding smoothly to their mastery, condoning no smallest breach of them, pursuing that, indeed, as far and as bitterly as vengeance may. It will be at no point a pretty picture. Set against it we have the cool comment of the neutral Senate House officials upon Marcius as he opens his political career:

> That's a brave fellow; but he's vengeance proud, and loves not the common people.
> Faith, there have been many great men that have flattered the people, who ne'er loved them; and there be many that they have loved, they know not wherefore: so that, if they love they know not why, they hate upon no better a ground. Therefore, for Coriolanus neither to care whether they love or hate him manifests the true knowledge he has in their disposition; and out of his noble carelessness lets them plainly see't.

'Noble carelessness'—that phrase alone, with what we have seen of him besides, would weight the sympathy well upon Marcius' side. But the yet cooler, the ironic

> but he seeks their hate with greater devotion than they can render it him . . .

caps it. A political play; the hero, under this aspect of it, with no more skill at the game than makes him his own worst enemy—a fruitful theme. Nor will he take counsel; Menenius could save him more than once. It is between him and the Tribunes that the earlier manoeuvring mostly proceeds; Marcius—if he would but let himself be so!—a glorious figurehead, the citizens poor puppets. And it is not so easy to pick holes in the Tribunes' conduct at first. They demand their people's rights: that is only their duty. Is it their fault if Marcius so grudgingly grants these? They slyly incite them to test him at his weakest point. Are they to blame if he not merely yields under the test, but unrepentingly proclaims that here he is, to their despite, at his strongest instead? It is something of a trap, but need he so recklessly walk into it?

But from now on they grow ever more contemptible. They promptly abuse the success they so easily win. Says Marcius scornfully,

> I do despise them;
> For they do prank them in authority
> Against all noble sufferance....
> It is a purposed thing, and grows by plot....

and—though they may safely deny it—we know this is true.

They overplay their hands when they demand Coriolanus' death, show their last sign of political good sense when they'd accept Menenius as mediator in the quarrel. Otherwise they had better have pressed for death, since exile is but to bring back revenge. And something of this they do actually, in the midst of the turmoil, perceive—

> To eject him hence
> Were but one danger, and to keep him here
> Our certain death....

—it being only that their insensate vanity, bred in the flush of success, so blinds them. Marcius gains tragic dignity in defeat and departure; they, tarring the rabble on to hoot him 'out at gates', swaggering ludicrously through the streets themselves—'our noble Tribunes'!— touch depth.

When the tide of fortune has turned, although we know what is coming, we see them still sunning themselves fatuously for a while

> i' the present peace
> And quietness o' the people . . .

Then, foolishly, futilely, denying the plain unpleasant fact, feebly protesting, when they cannot, against Menenius' mockery. Nor that the worst. While one still tries, and yet again, to argue facts away:

> *Enter a Messenger.*
> Sir, if you'd save your life, fly to your house:
> The plebeians have got your fellow-Tribune,
> And hale him up and down: all swearing, if
> The Roman ladies bring not comfort home,
> They'll give him death by inches.

Such politics have their revenges.

The Action of the Play

Enter a company of mutinous Citizens, with stones, clubs and other weapons.

BUT let not the unwary producer be led by that *mutinous*, and by the *stones, clubs and other weapons*, into projecting a scene of mere quick confusion, violence and high-pitched noise. Shakespeare has further reaching intentions. These citizens form a collective character, so to call it, of capital importance to the first half of the play; at its very start, therefore, we are to be given a fully informing picture of them. A homespun lot, but with a man or so among them that can both think and talk. They are certainly in an ugly temper at the moment and ripe for mischief, since plaints and a fortnight's threats have, it seems, proved futile; and they are not of the breed (Roman or British) that sits down to starve in patience. So if nothing is left them to do but to rid themselves and the world of this man they take to be their 'chief enemy', Caius Marcius—why, no more speech-making, nor parliamentary acclamations of 'Resolved, resolved!': let the thing be done! But they can be halted and made to listen yet once more. First it is to the chief rebel amongst them ruthfully justifying their intent, protesting that

> the gods know I speak this in hunger for bread, not in thirst for revenge. . . .

then to a last-minute defender Marcius finds among them, bidding them remember the 'services he has done for his country'. For even though he be 'a very dog to the commonalty', all that can be said for him must be heard.

The distant shouts of some kindred company of mutineers rouse them again; such temper is infectious. And they would be off to make common cause with these others; but Menenius Agrippa's arrival once again quiets them. They like old Menenius. He is 'one that hath always loved the people'. Even the First Citizen will grudgingly admit that

> He's one honest enough: would all the rest were so!

'Honest', perhaps; but little proof of his love for the people is in fact ever forthcoming, and the chief token

of his honesty would seem to be that he speaks his mind
bluntly to them. But he does so in a sort of rough good
fellowship, giving himself no high and mighty airs. How
far with them even a show of kindliness will go! He
knows how to tackle them. They are his 'countrymen',
his 'good friends', his 'honest neighbours'; and within a
few minutes he has this mutinous mob quietly gathered
round him while he tells them a fairy tale. It is the
parable of the Belly and the Members. Only that ruthful
rebel the First Citizen is mildly recalcitrant:

> you must not think to fob off our disgrace with a tale. . . .

—which, of course, is just what Menenius means to do.
And most readily he does it, going his own leisurely pace,
giving the homely humour its full value; and while he
holds them there absorbed the mutinous mood ebbs out
of them. With the recalcitrant First Citizen he spars
offhandedly. A dash of ironic flattery (but indeed the
creature is intelligent!), a tolerant snub, flooring him
finally amid the merriment of his fellows with a stroke
of something less than good-humoured ridicule:

> What do you think,
> You, the great toe of this assembly? . . .
> being one o' th' lowest, basest, poorest
> Of this most wise rebellion . . .

After which Caius Marcius himself—Coriolanus to be—
strides in.

It is for Shakespeare an unusual opening—the plays
offer indeed none comparable to it—with its hundred
and sixty lines of abortive revolt and elaborate parable;
he will habitually have swung his main theme into action
within half the time or less. But it accomplishes a variety
of purposes. The mutinous entry having furnished initial
impetus enough, its slackening, the debate, and their

equivocally mild response to Menenius' bluff bullying, give us a fair view of the citizens not yet in leash to their Tribunes, a sample of their native quality, upon which the lash of Marcius' contempt is next so precipitately to fall. The telling of the parable holds back the action, even as Menenius means it to hold up the revolt, yet bears directly on it, is no mere digression (that, at the play's outset, would be a weakness), but enlarges it at, so to say, one remove. This factor of the citizens and their condition is thus given ample preparatory display. Marcius' castigation will cow them now to silence. While the war with the Volsces is waging they will be absent from the scene. When they return to it Brutus and Sicinius will be their spokesmen, manoeuvring and colouring their cause for them.

Marcius, abruptly appearing, at once spurs the action to the swift pace his dominance of it befits. To Menenius' affectionately admiring tribute of a

> Hail, noble Marcius!

he—though young man to old—returns no more than a curt 'Thanks', so impatient is he to round on the mutineers. Plainly, Menenius' milder methods have already prevailed; but he must still vent his spleen. They are rogues and curs, hares in cowardice, geese in folly, ingrates, their own worst enemies, inconstant and perverse. They say, do they, that there is grain enough in the city, yet they are hungry, that though they be dogs, yet dogs must eat? But

> Would the nobility lay aside their ruth,
> And let me use my sword, I'd make a quarry
> With thousands of these quarter'd slaves, as high
> As I could pick my lance.

Doubtless! And all he says of them and more may be

true; but such scorn for starving fellow countrymen has no very chivalrous ring. Nor is Menenius' placatory

> Nay, these are almost thoroughly persuaded;
> For though abundantly they lack discretion,
> Yet are they passing cowardly.

the most generous comment possible upon their surrender to his wiles. Marcius, it may be, is the angrier with them since the other 'troops', whose shouts we heard, whom he has just quitted, have by their plaints prevailed with this same nobility to grant them

> a petition . . . a strange one . . .
> Five tribunes to defend their vulgar wisdoms . . .
>   S'death!
> The rabble should have first unroofed the city
> Ere so prevailed with me. . . .

He foresees, shrewdly enough, that

>   it will in time
> Win upon power and throw forth greater themes
> For insurrection's arguing.

There lies, indeed, the obstacle against which he is to bruise and break himself, and it is embryonic already in this group of sullen, silenced, confuted men over which he now rides so contemptuously roughshod. Marcius is about the least sympathetic of Shakespeare's heroes, and he is first shown to us in his unloveliest light.

He is happy to be freed from these cankerous domestic politics by the sudden news of war:

>   we shall ha' means to vent
> Our musty superfluity. . . .

And 'our best elders', whose coming follows the news—

Cominius the Consul, old Titus Lartius and other Senators—will have worthier duties to perform than playing
blackmail to the populace. He himself is consequently in
great credit:

> Marcius, 'tis true that you have lately told us;
> The Volsces are in arms.

He can smell the chance of a fight, from wherever the
wind of it blows. And at once, in sharp contrast, he is
at his best: his sword his country's, no questions asked;
chivalrous tribute paid to its chief enemy:

> Tullus Aufidius . . .
> $\qquad$ he is a lion
> That I am proud to hunt.

It may all go to a somewhat too self-sufficient tune, yet
pardonably stimulated, this—were stimulus needed—by
the deference Rome's great men offer him. He cannot
resist, moreover, a parting gibe at the 'worshipful mutiners', become sullenly silent onlookers, bidding them
follow him to play rats among the abundant Volscian
corn, which such a little valour will win. But, says the
stage direction,

> *Citizens steale away.*[11]

(the empty stomach not being one for fighting), while
Marcius, and old Titus, who'd

> lean upon one crutch and fight with t'other,
> Ere stay behind this business.

and Cominius the Consul and the Senators, depart
high-heartedly to the Capitol, their place of honour and
authority; from it to proclaim the war.

There have been two other onlookers, silent so far,

who now remain behind: Brutus and Sicinius, the newly appointed Tribunes. And in the twenty-five lines or so with which they finish the scene Shakespeare etches them in memorably for the caustic element in the play they are to prove; politicians sizing up their destined adversary and, dispassionately, cynically, the weakness and the strength of his position. Nothing to be done now. They must 'wait and see'.

THE VOLSCIANS

The succeeding scene shows us the Senators of Corioles in council of war, Aufidius bringing news to them of the Roman preparations, and receiving his commission as general in the field. The scene is but forty lines long; yet we learn besides that much 'intelligence' passes between Rome and the Volsces—a point to be made more than once; Rome, civilly distracted, has her fifth column—and from Aufidius, clinchingly, that

> If we and Caius Marcius chance to meet,
> 'Tis sworn between us we shall ever strike
> Till one can do no more.

The Senators are airily confident:

> Let us alone to guard Corioles. . . .

The clash is nearing.

With the scene which follows all the main factors of the play will have been assembled, and its opening stage direction is illuminating:

VOLUMNIA AND VIRGILIA

Enter Volumnia and Virgilia, mother and wife to Marcius.
They set them down on two low stools and sew.

This note of puritan simplicity is struck at once by nothing more elaborate than the two low stools and the sewing. For these are great ladies, and live in state, as the attendant Gentlewoman announcing the Lady Valeria, and the Usher and the Gentlewoman to show her in, will help show us within another minute or so.[12] We remark too the formality of their manners to each other in the 'sweet madam', 'good madam', 'my ladies both', 'your ladyship'. Volumnia dominates the household. It is to her that Valeria's visit is announced, and Virgilia asks her for permission to retire. Valeria, by contrast, will seem a very frivol; yet it is for a no wilder gaiety she would have Virgilia lay aside her 'stitchery' than to 'go visit the good lady that lies in'.

The scene gives us Volumnia's Spartan temper, harsh at its kindliest, her son's tones—his very words—echoing through hers; Virgilia's gentler spirit, her tremulous courage, her soft stubbornness; Valeria, witty and merry, primed with her news of the war. The opening prose is austere; it paints Volumnia. For the picturing of Marcius in the field comes coloured and moving verse. Valeria's chatter about the child brings prose again, easy and decorative, in which medium the scene ends. By reference, Valeria's news:

> the Volsces have an army forth; against whom Cominius the general is gone, with one part of our Roman power: your lord and Titus Lartius are set down before their city Corioles. . . .

advances us several steps in the war; and the next scene's opening:

> *Enter Marcius, Titus Lartius, with drum and colours, with*
> *Captains and Soldiers, as before the city Corioles.*

with the later

> *Enter two Senators with others on the walls of Corioles.*

THE WAR WITH THE VOLSCIANS:
BEFORE CORIOLES

—the walls being simply the upper stage—asks no further explanation.

The earlier scene has ended with a gentle little tussle between Valeria and Virgilia, and the gentler of the two has won. Now begins, under every form of contrast, the man's war. Marcius and Titus Lartius are in the highest spirits, the old soldier as youthful as the young, and laying bets—an English trait if not a Roman!—upon the news the Messenger, just sighted, will be bringing:

> A wager they have met
> My horse to yours, no?
> 'Tis done.
> Agreed.
> Say, has our general met the enemy?

and, the horse so sportingly lost and won, the bet is then, as between comrades, generously discounted.

This scene, and the three which follow, are to be predominantly scenes of action. Marcius is above all a fighting hero, and, most effectively to warrant him his title, Shakespeare lets us see him fight. Henry V, Antony, Othello, Macbeth, they also are soldiers; but—even with Henry V—that is not the aspect of them most vividly lighted. With Coriolanus, it is his personal prowess in war and its unlucky linking to as trenchant a pugnacity in peace that make and mar him. We have heard him for a start at his worst. We are now to see him at his best, winning valiantly to the summit of his fortunes. He will thus hold our regard the better along the descent to his tragic end.

For the battle without its walls, a Roman reverse and recovery, and the taking of Corioles; for a second wavering battle, Marcius to the rescue, and final victory, Shakespeare's material resources are little other than those of the old inn-yard, although doubtless the Globe Theatre at the height of its fame can enrich their quality and be more lavish with them. But *drum and colours* still sufficiently betoken an army on the march, and a recognized code of alarums, trumpet flourishes and the sounding of parleys and retreats illustrate the course of a battle or a siege. It is indeed only by the use of such tokens that the extension and swaying confusions of a battle can be made clear. For with hand-to-hand combat realism's limits are reached.

Shakespeare, using both speech and action, sets his board and makes his moves on it, with exactitude and economy. Marcius and Titus Lartius before Corioles learn that Cominius with his army facing the army of the Volsces are

> Within this mile and half.

Marcius' comment is that

> Then shall we hear their 'larum, and they ours.

When, therefore, a little later we hear the *Alarum afar off*, its meaning is at once plain to us, and distracting explanations are saved. For by then the Senators of Corioles are upon the walls, defying the Romans, and— as drums from within the city help inform us—about to anticipate their assault by a sortie. That Aufidius is not in the city we have at once been told. To the noise of the distant fight is added word that he is a captain in it. Marcius here, then, he there; they are not to meet yet.

> *Enter the army of the Volsces. . . . Alarum. The Romans*
> *are beat back to their trenches.*

The hiatus is filled by a seven-line speech from Marcius, both indicating and interpreting the accompanying action:

> They fear us not, but issue forth their city.
> Now put your shields before your hearts, and fight
> With hearts more proof than shields. . . .

That allows, if barely, the symbolic army time to enter and form line, the Romans to start to face them:

> Advance, brave Titus:
> They do disdain us much beyond our thoughts,
> Which makes me sweat with wrath. . . .

—impetuous, impatient!—

> Come on, my fellows:
> He that retires, I'll take him for a Volsce,
> And he shall feel mine edge.

rating them for cowards too, even by anticipation. Fighter but no leader! Then battle is joined and the Romans are beaten back.[13] After which

> *Enter Marcius, cursing.*

and the Romans rally; whether thanks to his magnificent vituperation we are free to judge. What is made plain, however, is that when he calls on them to follow him into the city in pursuit of the flying enemy—

> mark me, and do the like.

—none of them do. His is no way to win just such
devotion from his soldiers.

> Fool-hardiness; not I!
>> Nor I!

And when the gates close on him, for all comment
comes a

> See, they have shut him in.

with the grim humour of

> To the pot, I warrant him.

added. Then, Titus Lartius reappearing, Shakespeare
stages his great 'effect'. The gates open, and there stands
Marcius

> *bleeding, assaulted by the enemy.*

alone, at cut and thrust with the whole Volscian 'army';
and the amazing sight, and Titus Lartius' call to them,
shame the recalcitrant Romans—honest fighters enough
—into rescuing him, and so to taking the city.

The stage stays empty for a breathing-space. Then

> *Enter certain Romans, with spoils.*

and we have a three-line tokening of the customary sack
of a town:

> This will I carry to Rome.
> And I this.
> A murrain on 't! I took this for silver.

while the

> *Alarum continues still afar off.*

to remind us that Cominius and Aufidius, a 'mile and
half' away, are battling still. Marcius and Titus Lartius

return, Marcius fuller than ever of angry scorn for the common soldier, 'these movers . . . these base slaves' that

> Ere yet the fight be done, pack up. Down with them!

he cries, down with these paltry prizes they are pilfering.[14] The distant alarums continue.

> And hark, what noise the general makes! To him!
> There is the man of my soul's hate, Aufidius,
> Piercing our Romans: then, valiant Titus, take
> Convenient numbers to make good the city;
> Whilst I, with those that have the spirit, will haste
> To help Cominius.

His wounds still bleed. The veteran Titus counsels prudence, some respite. He will have none of that. He is off. Titus returns to the city.

The stage is again empty. Then

COMINIUS' PART OF THE BATTLE

Enter Cominius, as it were in retire, with soldiers.[15]

to a very different tempo.

> Breathe you, my friends; well fought! We are come off
> Like Romans, neither foolish in our stands,
> Nor cowardly in retire. . . .

Cominius is Consul and General in Chief, a steady, responsible soldier; and this has indeed quite the tone of an official bulletin, issued in mid-battle. For

> believe me, sirs,
> We shall be charged again. . . .

And news of Titus Lartius and Marcius is lacking, and when, long delayed, it comes, is bad. With clarity and economy Shakespeare connects the one fight and the other. Cominius has heard the alarums of the besiegers even as they have heard his. It is 'above an hour' since the Messenger left the Romans 'to their trenches driven'; and *we* know what has happened since then, and that Marcius himself is now upon his way here.[16] And when he arrives, so masked in blood that Cominius does not recognize him, we appreciate the effect to the full, since we have already seen him so, and it is as if we had a share ourselves in astonishing Cominius.

No more waiting now, with Marcius here, to be 'charged again', if he has aught to say in the matter.

> Where is the enemy? are you lords o' the field?
> If not, why cease you till you are so?

He has left Titus Lartius to do the 'mopping-up' in Corioles, is too impatient to be at it again to tell the story of the fight that is over, can scarce spare breath for further railing at 'the common file' he so detests. He begs to be set against Aufidius without more delay, and appeals for volunteers to follow him into what must prove a desperate struggle in nobler tones than have sounded from him yet:

> If any such be here,
> As it were sin to doubt, that love this painting
> Wherein you see me smeared; if any fear
> Lesser his person than an ill report;
> If any think brave death outweighs bad life
> And that his country's dearer than himself...

and—though momentarily touched by doubt of it when it comes—wins as generous a response.[17] Cominius, we note, without throwing more doubt upon its zeal, adds solid inducement:

Make good this ostentation, and you shall
Divide in all with us.

And so they march—thanks to Marcius, with fresh
spirit—to renew the fight.

BACK TO CORIOLES

Titus Lartius, having set a guard upon Corioles, going with
Drum and Trumpet toward Cominius and Caius Martius,
enters with a Lieutenant, other Soldiers and a Scout.

The scene's action and its seven spoken lines help—
and most economically—both to space out and knit
together the movements of the siege and the battle as a
whole, do so in time and place too. Titus Lartius gives
final orders to the Lieutenant for the holding of the town
and the sending of reinforcements for the battle still in
progress if they are needed. The Lieutenant retires within the gates, which are finally closed; and Titus Lartius
with his symbolic Drummer and Trumpeter, the Scout
for 'guider', and a selection of soldiers takes the road
that Marcius more hastily took a while before. The stage
is empty again. The curtains before the inner stage (and
the gates of Corioles) can now close.

BACK AGAIN TO COMINIUS' SIDE OF THE
BATTLE: CAIUS MARCIUS AND
AUFIDIUS MEET

Alarum as in battle.

—much such a sound as that which went with the fighting
under the walls, the Alarum afar off brought close, and
to its most startling and insistent. After which preparation.

Enter Marcius and Aufidius at several doors.

It is for each the peculiarly critical moment of the day. But before they come to blows they go to it with words, the one outscorning and outbragging the other. There is something of convention in this, doubtless; but it follows not so much Shakespeare's accustomed 'high Roman fashion' as that of Trojan and Greek in the scurril *Troilus and Cressida*. And it again gives us Marcius at his crudest, excusable by a certain boyishness in him, of character if not of years, of the unlicked cub in the man. Yet it is a flaw of character, which future subtler fighting than this will fatally widen. Nor is the outcome of this duel to prove lucky. Clean conquest of his enemy might serve him well. But

> *certain Volsces come in the aid of Aufidius.*

Marcius has little choice but to turn on them, and he

> *fights till they be driven in breathless.*

But for Aufidius to be left (since he can hardly make yet another in such a mêlée) to stand there a looker-on, or to follow after while Marcius so magnificently drives the fellows before him—

> Officious, and not valiant, you have shamed me
> In your condemned seconds.

—will he ever forgive that?[18]

THE VICTORIOUS ROMAN FORCES REASSEMBLE

Flourish. Alarum. A Retreat is sounded. Enter at one door Cominius with the Romans: at another door Marcius with his arm in a scarf.[19]

The battle is over. The strenuous beat of the action relaxes to the soberer measure of Cominius' stately praise.

The threads of the play's other themes begin at once to be woven back into the fabric. Cominius, addressing Marcius, speaks of

> the dull Tribunes
> That, with the fusty plebeians, hate thine honours...

Marcius, in deprecating response, of

> my mother,
> Who has a charter to extol her blood...

And here we have him at his best; not too mock-modestly belittling his own feats, genuinely generous to his comrades:

> I have done
> As you have done; that's what I can; induced
> As you have been; that's for my country:
> He that has but effected his good will
> Hath overta'en mine act.

rejecting reward without a second thought; acknowledging the supreme honour of

> For what he did before Corioles, call him,
> With all the applause and clamour of the host,
> Caius Marcius Coriolanus! Bear
> The addition nobly ever!

with humorous, becoming simplicity:

> I will go wash;
> And when my face is fair, you shall perceive
> Whether I blush or no: howbeit, I thank you.

Still more attractive is his plea amidst this triumph for the poor Volscian, some time his host, whose name he only finds himself too weary now to remember. He wants a drink of wine. And so we part from him, happy and magnanimous in victory; free too for the moment—or all but—from that self-conscious egotism which so besets him.

But the war is not to finish upon this note.

THE STANDPOINT OF THE VANQUISHED

A flourish. Cornets. Enter Tullus Aufidius, bloody, with two or three soldiers.[20]

Here are the defeated Volscians, and the shamed Aufidius. Cominius the Consul in the scene just past had ordered Titus Lartius back to Corioles, and from there to

> send us to Rome
> The best, with whom we may articulate,
> For their own good and ours.

But Aufidius scoffs at confidence in such a peace, in Rome's surrender of the conquered city:

> Condition!
> What good condition can a treaty find
> I' the part that is at mercy? Five times, Marcius . . .

—There it is!—

> I have fought with thee; so often hast thou beat me,
> And wouldst do so, I think, should we encounter
> As often as we eat.

From this sense that he will never now by fair means prove himself the better man springs the mistrust, and hatred, and will the treachery at last to come.

> My valour's poisoned
> With only suffering stain by him. . . .

—the keynote to Aufidius' spiritual tragedy, which time and the event are to work out.

ROME REJOICES

The entry of Menenius and the Tribunes, Sicinius and Brutus, shows that we are back in Rome. Their acrimonious banter—Menenius an expert at it, the other two doing their humourless best—opens a prospect of the civic war, which is to be rekindled now that the Volscian war is won. But the factors will differ, and the people, with the Tribunes to lead them, prove tougher combatants than before. We have a revaluing of the forces to be engaged, a fresh adjustment of sympathy. Menenius lures the two on. Marcius is blamed for his pride. But

> do you two know how you are censured here in the city, I mean of us o' the right hand file? do you? . . . You talk of pride: O! that you could turn your eyes toward the napes of your necks, and make but an interior survey of your good selves. O! that you could. . . . Why, then you should discover a brace of unmeriting, proud, violent, testy magistrates, alias fools, as any in Rome.

and then, before they can retort on him, he paints his own faults to his liking; an old trick in debate:

> I am known to be a humorous patrician, and one that loves a cup of hot wine with not a drop of allaying Tiber in 't. . . . What I think I utter, and spend my malice in my breath. . . .

with which excuse he goes on to tell them in comically coloured terms just what he thinks of them, of their exploiting of the people, and their pretentious folly in general:

> When you speak best unto the purpose, it is not worth the wagging of your beards; and your beards deserve not so honourable a grave as to stuff a botcher's cushion, or to be

entombed in an ass's pack-saddle. Yet you must be saying Marcius is proud.... God-den to your worships: more of your conversation would infect my brain....

And he turns from them, leaving them glowering, to accost Volumnia, Virgilia, Valeria—a high contrast, in dignity and beauty both—who are hastening across the stage. The news due tonight has come already (Shakespeare's habitual device for sharpening our expectation): the victorious army is approaching, with Marcius, who

comes the third time home with the oaken garland...

Acrid old Menenius transformed to a cheering schoolboy, his cap flung in the air; he and Volumnia, the two elders, competing in extravagant glee; Virgilia and Valeria the staider in joy, Virgilia shrinking from the thought of the wounds

I' the shoulder and i' the left arm: there will be large cicatrices to show the people when he shall stand for his place....

—this hint of what is to come another habitual device for the sharpening of our expectation. The Tribunes stay glowering in the background; Menenius cannot forbear a passing gibe at them. But suddenly from the distance comes a shout and the sound of trumpets, cutting sharply into the ferment of their jubilation: Volumnia, in a flash, responds; the Roman matron, and inspired:

Hark the trumpets!
These are the ushers of Marcius: before him he carries noise, and behind him he leaves tears:
Death, that dark spirit, in's nervy arm doth lie;
Which, being advanced, declines, and then men die.

A bold and masterly transition; from the familiar and excited prose of the exchanges with Menenius to the portentous trumpet-echoing

> These are the ushers of Marcius. . . .

and the measured music of the conventional 'sentence'.[21]

> *A sennet. Trumpets sound. Enter Cominius the general, and Titus Lartius; between them Coriolanus, crowned with an oaken garland, with Captains and Soldiers, and a Herald.*[22]

—with all possible pomp and circumstance, that is to say; and dialogue and stage direction now combine to make a notable and most eloquent effect. Nor is it eloquence of words alone; Shakespeare's stagecraft has outpassed that. Ringing speech pertains to the Herald:

> Know, Rome, that all alone Marcius did fight
> Within Corioles gates. . . .
> Welcome to Rome, renowned Coriolanus!

and to the response, in unison, of the nameless on-lookers:

> Welcome to Rome, renowned Coriolanus!

The flow of sound—trumpets, the Herald's trenchant tones, the volume of voices—suddenly ceasing, creates, so to speak, a silence in which Coriolanus' or Volumnia's simplest phrase, spoken in all simplicity, will tell to the height of its value.

> No more of this; it does offend my heart:
> Pray now, no more.

he begs them. The distaste is again genuine, barely tainted by mock-modesty. But the self-consciousness which sets him so continually insisting on it shows a crack in character, if a slight one.

The three women, becomingly, do not press forward; this, to the end, is soldiers' business. Cominius himself must intervene with a

> Look, sir, your mother!

And Marcius steps from his place of honour to kneel to her. For once her sterner self dissolves in emotion. There is tenderness in the pride of the

> Nay, my good soldier, up . . .

and thereupon he is her 'gentle' Marcius, her 'worthly' Caius, the pride returning almost shyly in the

> What is't? Coriolanus must I call thee?

as if she scarce dare trust the gloriously earned title on her tongue. Then she yields her mother's claim to the wife's.

Virgilia stands quietly, happily, crying. Marcius, to mask his own emotion at their reuniting, rallies her with a loving, but half-humorous

> My gracious silence, hail!

with the gentle irony of

> Wouldst thou have laughed had I come coffin'd home,
> That weep'st to see me triumph? . . .

The thought follows:

> Ah, my dear,
> Such eyes the widows in Corioles wear,
> And mothers that lack sons.

none better befitting the poignant gravity of such a triumph. It is Marcius' noblest moment.

Menenius recalls them to their rejoicings. These centre on this group of the people of consequence in Rome, exchanging greetings, so content with themselves and their world. Says Marcius:

> Ere in our own house I do shade my head
> The good patricians must be visited. . . .

He ignores, that is to say, the Tribunes, although Menenius, with another merry gibe, points them out to him. Volumnia voices more positively now her high hopes of the consulship for him. His response is cold. Then *Flourish. Cornets.* . . . , and the procession, Volumnia and Virgilia joined to it, passes on its way, leaving the neglected Brutus and Sicinius to discuss the situation.[23]

First, Brutus must vent his spleen. And if the colouring of his picture of Rome's greeting to her hero is dyed deep in jealousy of Marcius, it reflects contempt too for the people whose champion he is, as little kindness for 'the kitchen malkin' who

> pins
> Her richest lockram 'bout her reechy neck,
> Clambering the walls to eye him . . .

as for the 'seld-shown flamens' who 'press among the popular throngs' and 'our veiled dames' with 'their nicely-gawded cheeks'. A man of no rose-tinted illusions, Brutus, except, possibly, about himself!

Sicinius has his mind on realities. In a dry seven words he states them:

> On the sudden
> I warrant him Consul.

and Brutus, rancour indulged, is as shrewd:

> Then our office may,
> During his power, go sleep.

Very coolly the two then canvass the prospect: Marcius'
failings,

> He cannot temperately transport his honours. . . .

—the unstable temper of the commoners, which, in his
pride, he is sure soon to provoke again. So

> At some time when his soaring insolence
> Shall touch the people—which time shall not want,
> If he be put upon't; and that's as easy
> As to set dogs on sheep—will be his fire
> To kindle their dry stubble; and their blaze
> Shall darken him for ever.

They themselves have but meanwhile to 'suggest' to the
people—the word is twice used—

> in what hatred
> He still hath held them . . .

and wait, not for long.

The scene ends upon a Messenger's summoning them
to the Capitol, for

> 'Tis thought
> That Marcius shall be Consul. . . .

and he breaks, his commission done, into a rapturous

> I have seen the dumb men throng to see him, and
> The blind to hear him speak: matrons flung gloves,
> Ladies and maids their scarfs and handkerchers,
> Upon him as he passed; the nobles bended,
> As to Jove's statue, and the commons made
> A shower and thunder with their caps and shouts:
> I never saw the like.

It is Brutus' tale again, but by this young hero-wor-
shipper how differently told; its enthusiasm gall to the

hearers, who, bracing themselves for the coming
struggle, depart.

MARCIUS' FIRST STEP IN POLITICS

So much for the hero's greeting by his patrician equals
and by the populace. Shakespeare now provides a passing comment on him from a third standpoint.

Enter two Officers, to lay cushions, as it were, in the Capitol.[24]

Here is—to modernize it somewhat—the permanent
official's detached view of the politician, with its somewhat cynically critical discrimination. Coriolanus is

> a brave fellow; but he's vengeance proud, and loves not
> the common people.

Who, then, in Rome will not say that of him? Detached
analysis follows:

> there hath been many great men that have flattered the
> people, who ne'er loved them; and there be many that they
> have loved, they know not wherefore: so that if they love
> they know not why, they hate upon no better a ground.
> Therefore, for Coriolanus neither to care whether they love
> or hate him manifests the true knowledge he has in their
> disposition; and out of his noble carelessness lets them
> plainly see it.

True enough, and 'noble carelessness' no doubt becomes
a hero. But, comes the answer, is it only that?

> he seeks their hate with greater devotion than they can
> render in him, and leaves nothing undone that may fully
> discover him their opposite. Now, to seem to affect the
> malice and displeasure of the people is as bad as that which
> he dislikes, to flatter them for their love.

'He seeks their hate. . . .' Shrewd comment! And it is the seamy side of this aspect of the man, the impulse which sets him upon his road to disaster. For his defence:

> He hath deserved worthily of his country. . . .

and not to let such deeds excuse his faults were gross ingratitude. Finally, 'He's a worthy man'; on that they agree. Again—and here upon the verge of the action's chief struggle—Shakespeare has trimmed the balance of its sympathies.

Sennet. Enter, with Lictors before them, Cominius the Consul, Menenius, Coriolanus, Senators, Sicinius and Brutus. The Senators take their places; the Tribunes take theirs by themselves. Coriolanus stands.

The Lictors before the Consul, the Senators and Tribunes in their respective places, Coriolanus standing facing them, as one about to be harangued—this paints the occasion accurately enough; and Menenius' opening

> Having determined of the Volsces, and
> To send for Titus Lartius, it remains,
> As the main point of this our after-meeting . . .

enlarges the circumstances, and, by suggestion, lengthens the apparent time events have been taking, lending them more reality.[25]

Marcius is to be publicly thanked for his 'noble service' to the State. The question of the consulship, which is in everyone's mind, will be canvassed later, and with no voice to the contrary, supposedly, and so hard upon the praise with which Cominius will crown his triumph. Wherefore the Senators' confident request to the Tribunes, as 'Masters o' the people', for their 'kindest care', and their

> loving motion toward the common body,
> To yield what passes here.

But parliamentary courtesy between the parties is even now at a strain. Note Sicinius' canting

> We are convented
> Upon a pleasing treaty, and have hearts
> Inclinable to honour and advance
> The theme of our assembly.

continued smoothly into Brutus' sarcastic

> Which the rather
> We shall be blest to do, if he remember
> A kinder value of the people than
> He hath hereto prized them at.

and Menenius' temper tetchily shortening with these 'Masters o' the people' ('*your* people'—he cannot disguise his contempt). And while Cominius, ready with his Consular speech, is thus kept waiting, Coriolanus himself, hero of the occasion, declaring that

> I had rather have one scratch my head i' the sun
> When the alarum were struck than idly sit
> To hear my nothings monstered.

hardly improves it by abruptly departing. Altogether, an unpromising beginning to a political career!

But Cominius' speech, its recalling of what this man has done for Rome, must surely obliterate all petty differences about him. Says the chief Senator:

> He cannot but with measure fit the honours
> Which we devise him.

And when, brought back, Menenius announces to him without more ado:

> The Senate, Coriolanus, are well pleased
> To make thee Consul.

there is at least no dissentient voice. The business being on the crest of the wave, then, he adds at once—a monitory hint to Marcius, one fancies, in his tone:

> It then remains
> That you do speak to the people.

But—as is to be expected—without a moment's heed comes back the

> I do beseech you
> Let me o'erleap that custom. . . .[26]

and Sicinius is as quick with his

> Sir, the people
> Must have their voices; neither will they bate
> One jot of ceremony.

Menenius, however, all conciliation in success, would be closing the gap:

> Put them not to 't;
> Pray you, go fit you to the custom. . . .

And the self-conscious Marcius'

> It is a part
> That I shall blush in acting. . . .

is a yielding plea—were that all. But he must needs add:

> and might well
> Be taken from the people.

and play into the Tribunes' hands. Brutus'

> Mark you that!

is exultant. To cover the blunder and halt the dangerous argument, Menenius and the Senators, without more delay, in due form recommend him Consul to the

Tribunes, through them to the people, themselves, moreover, positively acclaiming him:

> to our noble Consul
> Wish we all joy and honour.

—and every voice in the Senate answers

> To Coriolanus come all joy and honour!

It is one of the play's salient and most significant
moments. Marcius has sworn (Brutus says he heard him,
reiterates, 'It was his word') that never, to be chosen
Consul, will he stand in the market place, show his
wounds and beg the people's voices. Yet plainly he now
means, after a little persuasion, to do so. Shakespeare
will not, in other words, bring him to grief upon a point
of mere stubbornness and vanity. And the Tribunes
would so far be facing defeat did he not in the very
same breath—and how gratuitously!—open up the larger
quarrel. Such a privilege

> might well
> Be taken from the people.

Thus jauntily he throws the gauntlet down. It is upon
what grows from this, issues of statecraft, nothing petty
and egotistic—however egotistically and arrogantly he
may urge them—that he will take his stand, and will
fail. Here is indeed the play's turning point, from which
it develops into true tragedy, with Marcius' character,
given that scope, itself rising to heroic stature.

The political war ahead, in which Coriolanus is to be
worsted, asks for other qualities than those which so well
served in him to beat the Volsces. Brutus and Sicinius
will prove to be the successful generals now, and their
tactics are to await for the while the adversary's errors.
The Senators and their hero departed; says Brutus,

You see how he intends to use the people.

And they set off themselves to anticipate Coriolanus in the market place and do what may seem wise to bias the proceedings there.[27]

THE TROUBLES IN THE MARKET PLACE BEGIN

Enter seven or eight Citizens.

In the few lines spoken before Marcius appears we renew acquaintance with them, and sample their present mood.

> Once, if he do require our voices, we ought not to deny him.

—the First Citizen is quite positive about it.[28] The Second Citizen insists on their rights:

> We may, sir, if we will.

The Third Citizen enjoys arguing things out, and the sound of words, and, possibly, of his own voice:

> We have power in ourselves to do it, but it is a power that we have no power to do.... Ingratitude is monstrous, and for the multitude to be ingrateful were to make a monster of the multitude....

They are not forgetful:

> for once we stood up about the corn, he himself stuck not to call us the many-headed multitude.

Yet they bear no malice; let bygones be bygones.

> if he would incline to the people, there was never a worthier man.

—upon which Marcius appears, as demanded, in the gown of humility, shepherded by a Menenius who is plainly most apprehensive of what may happen when in a moment his fatherly and restraining influence is withdrawn.

As with the scenes of battle, the passages which now follow between Coriolanus and the citizens are as eloquent, or all but, in their action as in their speech; and disposition and movement ask careful perceiving. Both parties at first shirk the encounter. The citizens, at the sight of the man who has heretofore never met with them but to abuse them, herd together for mutual support, until the sapient Third Citizen protests that

> We are not to stay all together, but to come to him where he stands, by ones, by twos and by threes. . . .

and stiffens their backs a bit. And Coriolanus, that bold fighter, at his most miserably self-conscious as he shows himself in the detested gown, would bolt, it seems, from these despised boors if he might, like a shy schoolboy. There is a generous measure of the comic in the scene, contributed by no means by its simpletons only. Shakespeare does not scruple now, should it suit him, to add to a tragic hero's diet a taste or two of the bitter sauce of ridicule.

Coriolanus takes his stand, to await assault. It is a queer caricature of the picture we so recently had of him, fighting 'all alone . . . within Corioles gates'. He now has instead of Volsces these kindly fumbling fellow Romans, offering him a victory which the arrogant demon in him does everything to spurn. Fatherly Menenius is in despair:

> You'll mar all:
> I'll leave you: pray you, speak to 'em, I pray you,
> In wholesome manner.

and Marcius' response is certainly not reassuring:

> Bid them wash their faces,
> And keep their teeth clean.

—let them hear it if they like; what does he care!²⁹

It looks, indeed, an embarrassing business enough: the hero, stripped of his martial trappings, his oaken garland, and appearing, it must be owned, a little ridiculous in this gown of humility. Not so ridiculous as he himself fears, and in the eyes of these simple, serious-minded citizens, not at all. But Marcius, his martial glory disregarded, has not—it is the fatal flaw—the humane and inward dignity which can outshine appearances.

It is distressing, also, to see him so smartly sparring at these simple folk, unable to resist the puzzling repartee, the adroit seizing of a vantage-point, the covert insolence. One gentle stroke pierces his harness. The Third Citizen has ventured the artlessly cunning, joke-in-earnest of

> You must think, if we give you anything, we hope to gain by you.

upon which Marcius pounces with

> Well then, I pray, your price o' th' consulship?

Says the First Citizen very quietly:

> The price is to ask it kindly.

That goes home. It does not soften him. He is no sentimentalist. But at least he next responds as one man allowably may to another—

> Kindly! Sir, I pray, let me ha't: I have wounds to show you, which shall be yours in private. Your good voice, sir; what say you?

—if, even so, he cannot keep derision from his tones, inverted arrogance from the concluding

> I have your alms. Adieu!

They have not the wit nor the wish to retort on him in kind. But they are none the less conscious of his mockery, and resentment will secrete in them only the more abundantly.

These three are replaced by a Fourth Citizen and a Fifth, the Fourth plain-spoken:

> You have deserved nobly of your country, and you have not deserved nobly. . . . You have been a scourge to her enemies, you have been a rod to her friends; you have not indeed loved the common people.

The candidate counters with irony:

> You should account me the more virtuous that I have not been common in my love. . . .

But by all means, if they prefer it, he will flatter his

> sworn brother the people, to earn a dearer estimation of them . . . practise the insinuating nod . . . counterfeit the bewitchment of some popular man, and give it bountiful to the desirers. . . .

Could he—were they not such impervious clods!—do more positively to induce them to reject him? Nor will he frankly show these two his wounds; only, since he must, beg them for their 'voices'—which they promise him 'heartily'. He is then left a breathing-space.

Marcius is no more given to reasoning coolly with himself than with others. Inward conviction is his only strength; and, erring against it, as he is erring now, he becomes like an animal caught in a net, frantic, struggling, self-strangled.

> Better it is to die, better to starve . . .

—by test of reason, certainly, a somewhat overcharged outburst. The protest against custom's tyranny,

> What custom wills, in all things should we do't,
> The dust on antique time would lie unswept,
> And mountainous error be too highly heaped
> For truth to o'erpeer. . . .

comes with unconscious irony from the conservative mind in rebellion. But, having brought himself thus far to 'fool it so'—

> I am half through;
> The one part suffered, the other will I do.

—resentment would seemingly fade into shrugging self-contempt, did there not at this point

Enter three Citizens more.

The sight of them stirs him to a very self-scourging of mockery:

> Your voices! For your voices I have fought;
> Watched for your voices; for your voices bear
> Of wounds two dozen odd; battles thrice six
> I have seen and heard of. . . .

But, their own stolid simplicity unaffected, the scourge flags, the mockery peters out—

> for your voices have
> Done many things, some less, some more: your voices. . . .

—into the final surrender of

> Indeed, I would be Consul.

That he should come to this! They give him his reward:

> He has done nobly. . . . Therefore let him be Consul. . . .
> God save thee, noble Consul!

and as Menenius returns, the Tribunes with him, these simple folk inconspicuously depart; Marcius, released, venting an incorrigible

> Worthy voices![30]

Menenius is triumphant. His man wins; and the rest of the business can be pushed through without more delay. Sicinius stiffly assents. Marcius only demands: will it be decently done in the Senate House, not here in the vulgar market place; and

> May I change these garments?

—this ridiculous 'gown of humility'? He may. Then all's well; and he and Menenius both are off in high feather. Diplomatic Menenius does not forget to ask their good colleagues the Tribunes to go along with them. No; they prefer to 'stay here for the people'; their people. Sicinius' smooth 'Fare you well' has an inauspicious ring.

Brutus thinks all is lost for the time being, and would dismiss the people. Sicinius will wait and see. And, sure enough, when the plebeians reassemble, the tide of their favour towards Marcius is already on the turn. Did he suppose, because they did not retort then and there, that they were insensible to his sarcasm?

> To my poor unworthy notice,
> He mocked us when he begged our voices.

says the Second Citizen; and the Third, thus encouraged:

> Certainly.
> He flouted us downright.

But attack again brings defence. The First Citizen, in a minority of one though he may be, stands out:

> No, 'tis his kind of speech; he did not mock us.

As in that old quarrel over the corn, Marcius must have fair play.

Brutus and Sicinius know better than to join in the attack while it is strong enough without them. There are better ways of fomenting it. Surely he can never have refused—Sicinius won't believe it—his fellow citizens their right to see

> His marks of merit, wounds received for 's country.

The Third Citizen is effectively roused:

> He said he had wounds, which he could show in private;
> And with his hat, thus waving it in scorn,
> 'I would be consul', says he: 'aged custom,
> But by your voices, will not so permit me;
> Your voices therefore.'

Not a derisive phrase nor a scornful twist of the tongue did he miss, it seems:

> When we granted that,
> Here was, 'I thank you for your voices: thank you:
> Your most sweet voices: now you've left your voices
> I have no further with you.' Was not this mockery?

The rest mutely agree. They have behaved like fools. The Tribunes now read them—and not for the first time, upon this very subject!—a sound political lesson.[31]

Admitting that his recent 'worthy deeds' gave him a claim upon them, they should have reminded him of his ancient enmity towards them. Clearly, they should have said, they could not risk his remaining a 'fast foe to the Plebeii'. They should indeed have demanded from him a pledge for his future good behaviour—which, if he had given it, they could have held him to; and if, as was more likely, the mere demand had 'galled his surly nature', then, 'putting him to rage', they could have

> ta'en the advantage of his choler,
> And passed him unelected.

For do they suppose that a man who can treat them as he has now done when he needs their votes will prove very considerate when he no longer needs them? And are they, who have ' 'ere now denied the asker'—the candid, honest asker—to bestow their 'sued-for tongues' in thanks for such treatment as this? The appeal is to sound sense and self-respect. And it needs but a single evasive·

> He's not confirmed; we may deny him yet.

to stampede the rest:

> And will deny him:
> I'll have five hundred voices of that sound.

And the rot will spread:

> I twice five hundred and their friends to piece 'em.

Brutus has the demagogue's sense of a crowd's mood and the critical moment:

> Get you hence instantly, and tell those friends,
> That they have chosen a Consul that will from them take
> Their liberties. . . .

—rate them for fools as we are rating you. But Sicinius is for putting a more temperate face on the affair:

> Let them assemble,
> And, on a safer judgment, all revoke
> Your ignorant election. . . .

—let them confess it to be so. Then he builds them up their case; against Marcius' pride, and his old hatred of them, which in the light of his great deeds they had been so ready to forget as not to note the mocking scorn, sure sign that he hated them still. Upon which draft Brutus is quick to improve:

> Lay
> A fault on us, your Tribunes, that we laboured—
> No impediment between—but that you must
> Cast your election on him.

A brilliant manoeuvre from the Tribunes' standpoint! The people will save their faces, and they win credit for a patriotic effort to heal this old unhappy quarrel. So excellent seems the notion that they enlarge on it until they find themselves lauding, not Marcius alone, but his ancestors also for their services to Rome and its people; very practical, popular services; for

> Of the same house Publius and Quintus were,
> That our best water brought by conduits hither. . . .

So Sicinius must steer back to the point, that

> you have found . . .
> That he's your chief enemy, and revoke
> Your sudden approbation.

while Brutus encourages them again with another

> Say you ne'er had done it—
> Harp on that still—but by our putting on. . . .

for already the tide of their resentment has ebbed to the uncertainty of an

> *almost* all
> Repent in their election.

But they depart to do the bidding of these political masters, who linger a moment, themselves, before taking their shorter way to the Capitol, to reflect that, mildly as it yet promises,

> This mutiny were better put in hazard
> Than stay, past doubt, for greater. . . .

and that, arriving 'before the stream of the people', the threat of it can be made to

> seem, as partly 'tis, their own,
> Which we have goaded onward.

THE BATTLEGROUND IS BEFORE THE CAPITOL NOW

Cornets. Enter Coriolanus, Menenius, all the Gentry,
Cominius, Titus Lartius, and other Senators.

All the Gentry is to be noted, with the completeness of the contrast it indicates between this gathering and that of the home-spun group of citizens. The cornets, elaborately sounding, tell us that the ceremonies of the election are not yet over. Coriolanus is once more fitly attired for them. And he is already deferred to as Consul—Titus Lartius, back from Corioles, but still in fighting trim, calls him 'my lord'; Cominius addresses him as 'Lord Consul'—and spontaneously, confidently, so asserts himself. He nurses no illusions, as the more pacific Cominius does, that Rome has finished with the Volscians, points a prompt finger towards the source of trouble to come with his

> Saw you Aufidius?

is as boyishly himself as ever in the eager

                    Spoke he of me? . . .
                              How? What?

Aufidius has retired to Antium, has he, there to bide his
time? This by triple repetition is impressed on us. Then,
says Marcius:

 I wish I had a cause to seek him there. . . .

—and the words will lodge in our memory.

So here is Coriolanus on the very crest of the wave,
Rome's leader-elect, and just such a leader as she may
most need, with war, as is hinted, likely to threaten her
again. Supported by the Senate and the gentry, he is
now on his way back from the Capitol to the market
place for the final act of the election, the people's
confirmation of their acceptance of him. The Tribunes
enter as from the market place. They do not speak at
once; and Marcius apparently is not unwilling that, as
they stand there, they should overhear his comments on
them:

 Behold, these are the tribunes of the people,
 The tongues o' the common mouth: I do despise them;
 For they do prank themselves in authority,
 Against all noble sufferance.[32]

The Tribunes do not mean to be provoked into losing
their tempers. They are come, on the contrary, to pre-
vent disorder. Coriolanus must not proceed to the market place:

 The people are incensed against him.

Brutus confirming Sicinius with a solemn

         Stop,
 Or all will fall in broil.

Coriolanus, needless to say—and the Tribunes have counted on it—flares into anger at once, and first against the Tribunes themselves for failing to control their 'herd':

> What are your offices?
> You being their mouths, why rule you not their teeth?

'Rule'—the first thought to his mind; and a minute later he is inveighing against

> such as cannot rule
> Nor ever will be ruled.

(Brutus and Sicinius could tell him if they would that while they get their own way with their 'herd'—and better than he knows how to—it is not by rule.)

His tactic, in this sort of fight as in another, is at once to force the acutest issue:

> Have you not set them on?

—let them deny it if they can. Theirs is to lure him aside. The vexed, one-time question about the corn, Brutus neatly casts that into the arena. Marcius scoffs:

> Why, this was known before.

and—the quarrel then widening to admit Cominius and Menenius to a share in it—one hopes he may have the sense to drop the subject. But no!

> Tell me of corn!
> This was my speech, and I will speak 't again—

and not Menenius nor the Senators can stay him.

Nor is this the worst. Though his friends beseech him not to, he must needs go on to raise the whole question of these privileges that have been granted to 'the mutable, rank-scented meynie'—political disapproval and personal fastidiousness combined!—for

> I say again,
> In soothing them we nourish 'gainst our Senate
> The cockle of rebellion, insolence, sedition,
> Which we ourselves have ploughed for, sowed and scattered,
> By mingling them with us, the honoured number. . . .

Brutus' acid comment,

> You speak o' the people
> As if you were a god to punish, not
> A man of their infirmity.

is a not altogether surprising one.

Marcius had been ready with this protest, and was fended by but a little from making it, upon the verge of the prescribed appeal in the gown of humility on the market place. In hot blood he has, to their faces, denounced the people yet more fiercely; and Menenius urges the Tribunes not, in fairness, to take advantage of his choler now. Marcius consents to no such excuse:

> Choler!
> Were I as patient as the midnight sleep,
> By Jove, 't would be my mind.

And it is at this juncture that, a graver note sounding, we become aware of him grown to more heroic stature, to take his stand for a cause of greater import than his own:

> O good, but most unwise patricians! why,
> You grave but reckless Senators, have you thus
> Given Hydra here to choose an officer . . . ?

For of two things one: the hydra-headed people will rule, or he—this Sicinius or the like—in their name; and

> If he have power,
> Then veil your ignorance; if none, awake

> Your dangerous lenity. If you are learned,
> Be not as common fools; if you are not,
> Let them have cushions by you. You are plebeians,
> If they be Senators: and they are no less. . . .
> > By Jove himself,
> It makes the Consuls base: and my soul aches
> To know, when two authorities are up,
> Neither supreme, how soon confusion
> May enter 'twixt the gap of both and take
> The one by the other.

—it is a note never sounded by Marcius before; the rare note of selfless intellectual passion.

This is the juncture too at which he begins to alienate his friends. Little do the Senators want less—they are as apt politicians as the Tribunes—than to have such an issue raised. Cominius would evade it with a

> Well, on to the market place.

But that only sets this incorrigible Consul-elect to prove his case by revising the well-worn quarrel about the corn—and, since he will, why, adroitly he argues it as could the most proficient politician of them all. And that brings him to lashing at the people yet once more for their wartime cowardice, and Menenius cannot stop him.

He finds himself at last upon the higher ground again, for him the highest. What can go well in a state

> where gentry, title, wisdom,
> Cannot conclude but by the yea and no
> Of general ignorance . . .

Even for the people's own sake

> at once pluck out
> The multitudinous tongue; let them not lick
> The sweet which is their poison. . . .

Dangerous ground! Brutus and Sicinius have no more need of their façade of indignation. It sputters from them:

> Has said enough.
> Has spoken like a traitor, and shall answer
> As traitors do.

But it is not in Marcius to retreat. Here, indeed, he is, in the sort of situation that most delights him, single-handed against odds, reckless of consequence. And with the happy, schoolboy ribaldry of the question:

> What should the people do with these bald Tribunes. . . ?

he is ready to

> throw their power i' the dust.

Not for this was he to be elected Consul. It is, as Brutus says, 'Manifest treason'. But revolutions do not always come from below.

Such a quarrel started, each must line up on his own side. And the summoning of the Aediles to apprehend Rome's hero

> as a traitorous innovator,
> A foe to the public weal . . .

—the Tribunes will carefully keep their law-abiding and conservative footing—rallies the troubled Senate round him.[33] Sicinius, violently excited, is for arresting Marcius with his own hands; Cominius, scandalized, protesting; Marcius, at his senile touch, with a

> Hence, rotten thing, or I shall shake thy bones
> Out of thy garments.

sending him yelping off in terror. Hullaballoo ensues; Coriolanus alone standing silent and unmoved:

The first thing is to quiet it; and this only the Tribunes, who have roused it, can well do. Menenius, outshouted, helpless, is reduced to begging 'good Sicinius' to speak to the people. If he thinks he has a peacemaker in him he is much mistaken. Sicinius but repeats quietly and more clearly what he has already called aloud:

> You are at point to lose your liberties:
> Marcius would have all from you; Marcius,
> Whom late you have named for Consul.

And to the shocked reproach from the Senate side that

> This is the way to kindle, not to quench.
> To unbuild the city and to lay all flat.

he launches at Marcius, who would throw the popular power 'in the dust', the tit-for-tat

> What is the city but the people?

with its powerful chorus of popular response:

> True,
> The people are the city.

And thus can the political pendulum swing once it is started swinging.

For the Tribunes, cooler now and confident with their followers ranged behind them, this is a chance not to be missed, of pushing their power to its utmost. It marks them and their kind that they cannot resist the temptation. Their enemy, attacking them, has rashly talked treason too; and, says Sicinius:

> This deserves death.

Brutus adds categorically,

> Or let us stand to our authority
> Or let us lose it. We do here pronounce
> Upon the part o' the people, in whose power
> We were elected theirs, Marcius is worthy
> Of present death.

And, without more ado, the sentence ends, he is to be flung from the Tarpeian rock. Menenius—violence imminent, his side outnumbered—beseeches lenity. Marcius, silent till now, simply draws his sword, and says,

> No, I'll die here.

He adds, more sportingly,

> There's some among you have beheld me fighting:
> Come, try upon yourselves what you have seen me.

Urged by the Tribunes, they tumultuously do; and

In this mutiny, the Tribunes, the Aediles, and the People, are beat in.

—as, with Marcius at the head of even a handful of men of good fighting quality (Cominius is there, and Titus Lartius), such a rabble might look to be.

But it is to be noted how the impromptu victory is taken: Menenius' first thought is for Marcius to profit from it by retreating to his house and leaving the reasonable rest of them to patch up the best peace they can. One or two are left fighting keen.[34] But

> Shall it be put to that?

—Romans at war with Romans—

> The gods forbid!

In affection for his hero the old man mitigates the effect of Marcius' grimly vaunting

> On fair ground
> I could beat forty of them.

with the humour of his own

> I could myself
> Take up a brace o' the best of them; yea, the two Tribunes.

But it is a relief to have him gone. Comment is practical:

> This man has marred his fortune.

—this is *not* the way to campaign for the consulship in Rome.[35]
And through Menenius' loyally laudatory

> His nature is too noble for the world:
> He would not flatter Neptune for his trident,
> Or Jove for's power to thunder....

can be heard, perhaps, the man of the world's sigh of exasperation at being left to clear up if he can the mess this noble nature has made of things. It issues in a final

> What the vengeance!
> Could he not speak 'em fair?

But a breathing-space at least has been gained, in which Menenius himself can 'speak 'em fair', can try, as he said,

> whether my old wit be in request
> with those that have but little . . .

and here we may recall our first sight of him at the play's opening, and the skill with which he quieted the mutiny over the corn. This is a harder task. Brutus and Sicinius are not to be so cajoled. They possess authority, moreover, to which he takes care to show deference, while Marcius has put himself indefensibly in the wrong. And the people are for the moment—wherefore the Tribunes are astutely demanding death without delay—authentically incensed against him, witness the full chorus of reiterated 'No, no...' which greets his mere tentative naming as 'the Consul Coriolanus'. He must make for him, then, must Menenius, such a place with the people as the Tribunes dare not, for shame—will not, for policy—obstruct.

First, it is to a regard for Rome's good name:

> whose gratitude
> Towards her deserved children is enrolled
> In Jove's own book...

Then:

> What has he done to Rome that's worthy death?
> Killing our enemies, the blood he hath lost—
> Which, I dare vouch, is more than that he hath,
> By many an ounce—he dropped it for his country;
> And what is left, to lose it by his country
> Were to us all, that do 't and suffer it,
> A brand to the end o' the world.

'Were to us all'—they are one in citizenship with him, and all are Rome.

The Tribunes see that they must put a stop to this, must let loose the pent wrath of the people, before, under such soothing, it abates altogether. But—each minute a gain—Menenius begs for

> One word more, one word.

And of full effect he makes it; with its warning whither 'tiger-footed rage' may lead, his repicturing to the people of their soldier

> bred i' the wars
>> Since he could draw a sword ...

and his final promise to bring him back to them com-
pliant in spirit. And the Senatorial

>> Noble Tribunes,
> It is the humane way. ...

solidly supports him.

They are practised politicians, are the Tribunes, and
can quickly tack and veer, and turn moderation to
account as well as rage. If they do not now give Marcius
another chance, they may well, under the effect of such
appeals for him, split their own party. If they do, and
he does not take it, he will probably split his own, and
they will have him the more at their mercy. Besides,
Menenius will almost certainly fail to bring him tamely
to heel. So Sicinius generously consents; a touch of
sardonic humour in his

>> Noble Menenius,
> Be you, then, as the people's officer ...

And the

> Masters, lay down your weapons.
>> Go not home.
> Meet on the market place. ...

is but a menace postponed. To Menenius and the Senators, indeed, Sicinius is coldly explicit:

> Where, if you bring not Marcius, we'll proceed
> In our first way.

Menenius' 'old wit' has won him somewhat; but despite the jovially confident

> I'll bring him to you.

he knows how precariously little yet. And the scene ends upon the ominous muted note of his

> He must come,
> Or what is worst will follow.

as he and the Senators depart to fulfil the no easier second half of their task—if they can!

Coriolanus absent, and his violent stimulus to the action lacking, its pulse has kept a steadier beat. There is no slackening, the tension is sustained; and we are stirred to question: will he once more yield to persuasion, or no?

VOLUMNIA'S SHARE IN THE QUARREL

Finding him at his house, the young nobility around him, high-mettled and wilful as he, truly it does not seem likely.[36] He is at the highest pitch of indignant wrath:

> Let them pull all about mine ears; present me
> Death on the wheel, or at wild horses' heels;
> Or pile ten hills on the Tarpeian rock
> That the precipitation might down stretch
> Below the beam of sight; yet will I still
> Be thus to them.

flattered in it by these young supporters of his own breed and mind whom conflict begins to gather to him—one of them exclaiming,

> You do the nobler.

—pricked the more to it by a most unexpected crossing just encountered:

> I muse my mother
> Does not approve me further...

We may note how Shakespeare here concentrates his action, dovetails it, coils it like a spring to give it strength. Marcius left the Capitol with Cominius, who has now, apparently, gone elsewhere; we shall learn where and why later. He himself has been at home long enough for a first encounter with Volumnia, the result of it shown in the outburst with which the scene opens, the violent recoil from her sober counsel; and that this *is* the result of it to be surmised from the sight of her as she slowly follows him and stands, disapproval in her attitude, until he turns to discover and ask,

> Why did you wish me milder?[37]

Here too the depicting of Marcius takes a more intimate turn. Man of action, of impulse, and of quick response to his fellows whether in anger or affection, we do not find him reflecting in solitude. Shakespeare allots him but one short soliloquy, and that to mark his loneliness and defeat.[38] He is brought nearest to consciousness of himself—the boyish self-consciousness that plagues him a very different thing!—when he looks, as now, in the glass of his mother's opinion of him. This has been satisfyingly flattering so far; he 'muses' the more that she should now wish him to be false to himself. And the tragedy of character gains shape.

He yielded to persuasion and was false to himself when he put on the gown of humility and stood begging for votes in the market place. But at least he did it ill; and he atoned to himself, moreover, when the chance came, by giving Tribunes and people a fuller taste of his true mind than otherwise he would have done—gave it to his own prejudice too. This new temptation to go back upon himself finds him at first more violent in resistance, yet the less able to resist.

Having vented in defiance his astonishment that Volumnia should so rebuke him, he listens to her respectfully, lovingly; to Menenius and the Senators, coming in hope and doubt from their parley with the Tribunes; to Cominius, who later reports from the market place that the issue must be faced—to all their politic advice. But it is a chilling change from his mother's accustomed fervours to the biting

> You might have been enough the man you are
> With striving less to be so. . . .

apt and deserved though this may be. That he is right in what he has said, but that he should wait, should he, to say it until those that hold him wrong are in his power?—it is foxy doctrine. He has been, protests genial old Menenius, 'too rough, something too rough. . . .' From Volumnia, again, who claims for herself

> a brain that leads my use of anger
> To better vantage.

(not that, tested so little later, this appears) he faces a

> You are too absolute.

He, then, their hero, if he is to be their Consul, has some most unheroic lessons to learn. To return to the Tribunes and publicly repent what he has spoken— which he would not do to the gods! But he listens still. He has no taste for argument. Strange that it should be his mother cleverly proving to him, his friends applauding, that a lie told to his fellow Romans here to gain his ends no more dishonours him than it would in war thus

> to take in a town with gentle words,
> Which else would put you to your fortune and
> The hazard of much blood . . .

But a good argument doubtless. Not a very admirable picture, though, that she sketches of him for his copying:

> with this bonnet in thy hand . . .
> Thy knee bussing the stones—for in such business
> Action is eloquence, and the eyes of the ignorant
> More learned than the ears—waving they head,
> (Which often) thus correcting thy stout heart,
> Now humble as the ripest mulberry
> That will not hold the handling. . . .

And, even more than in his donning of the gown of humility, does it put him to a part which, he protests, he never can 'discharge to the life'. But, waging this sort of war, his friends have him at their mercy as never had his enemies when he faced *them* sword in hand. For his wife's sake, his son's, in the Senators' cause and the nobles', it is his duty, so it seems, to forswear himself. And Volumnia, argument unavailing, coaxes and chides him like a child, and, as a last resource, treats him to a hot fit of the very temper she has so disastrously bred in him.

He is swung from a baited

> Well, I must do 't.

and from his own yet sorrier filling-in of her sorry picture of him—

> Away, my disposition, and possess me
> Some harlot's spirit! my throat of war be turned,
> Which quired with my drum, into a pipe
> Small as an eunuch . . .
> a beggar's tongue
> Make motion through my lips, and my armed knees,
> Who bowed but in my stirrup, bend like his
> That hath received an alms! . . .

—to the violent revolt of

> I will *not* do 't
> Lest I surcease to honour mine own truth,

And by my body's action teach my mind
A most inherent baseness.

but, finally, as she rounds on him, to a boylike

> Pray, be content,
> Mother, I am going to the market place;
> Chide me no more. . . .

It is the endearing side of him.

> I'll mountebank their loves,
> Cog their hearts from them, and come home beloved
> Of all the trades in Rome. Look, I am going:
> Commend me to my wife. . . .

The invincible soldier! Vulnerable in the simplicity of his affections, as son, husband, father, friend! Pure patriot, by his unquestioning lights; his life his country's! As a politician, a fool!

He is foredoomed to fail in this coming test, with which the long strain of his campaign for the consulship is to end. It does not lie in him to be cynically false to his nature. He knows only how to be true even to its faults. Still, he will please them if he can; to have his mother turn her back on him in anger distresses him. So, with 'Mildly' for his watchword—a wry irony evolving from the sound of it as he and Menenius pass it between them—he sets out again at the head of his party.

BANISHMENT

Sicinius and Brutus (the appointment was for the market place; when we see them enter, then, we shall presume them there) have not wasted time. While Senators and nobles have been at odds with their candidate and leader, they, by contrast, have been drilling their followers and developing their tactics. Coriolanus can still be best accused of aiming at tyrannical power; and, says Brutus,

> In this point charge him home. . . .

But 'if he evade us there. . . ', if, that is to say, Menenius has succeeded in making him see reason, why, to tax him with having, in his hatred for the people, deprived them of their share of the spoil 'got on the Antiates', will certainly rouse his wrath again. He is coming, they hear; accompanied, of course, by old Menenius

> and those Senators
> That always favoured him.

There are others, then; and his party can be divided. Then come their last-minute instructions to the Aedile. The people have been organized in their legal groups? Good. Let them listen for their leaders' voices; and, says Sicinius,

> when they hear me say 'It shall be so
> I' the right and strength o' the Commons', be it either
> For death, for fine, or banishment, then let them
> If I say fine, cry 'fine', if death, cry 'death'. . . .

—for only with such docile followers can a democratic leader do himself full credit, reap the moment's maximum harvest. But there are, besides, the opposite uses to which a crowd can be put:

> And when such time they have begun to cry,
> Let them not cease, but with a din confused
> Enforce the present execution. . . .

Then Brutus, kindling to the opportunity:

> Put him to choler straight.

and the rest will follow. The unhappy Coriolanus is no better than a child in their hands. Sicinius, beneath the surface, is as excited:

> Well, here he comes.

It is a tense and a pregnant moment.

Menenius, on the way here, has been harping, seemingly, on the single string, its note varied only from the parting 'Mildly' to this

> Calmly, I do beseech you.

—Marcius' muttered answer not reassuring! The opponents face each other like duelists with a ceremonious salute; and what could be more exemplary than Marcius'

> The honoured gods
> Keep Rome in safety, and the chairs of justice
> Supplied with worthy men! plant love among's!
> Throng our large temples with the shows of peace,
> And not our streets with war!

Menenius applauds, as might a proud tutor his pupil:

> A noble wish!

The Tribunes duly proceed:

> Draw near, ye people.

And the Aedile sustains their dignity:

> List to your Tribunes! Audience! Peace, I say!

Now comes manoeuvring for position. Is this to be the end of the dispute? Marcius demands; Sicinius in turn:

> If you submit you to the people's voices,
> Allow their officers, and are content
> To suffer lawful censure for such fault
> As shall be proved upon you?

'Submit . . . censure . . . faults . . .'; it is a bitter pill. The Tribunes hope, the Senators fear, that he will never swallow it. With a Spartan

> I am content.

he does. Upon which, his friends cannot in prudence but see, the business had best be brought to a quick finish. Yet Menenius, though he himself sees it—

> Lo! citizens, he says he is content. . . .

—cannot resist pleading once more the cause that is already won, so well has he pleaded it; the advocate's common fault! 'Warlike service' and 'wounds' must again be commended; and Marcius himself, as before, must mock-modestly protest,

> Scratches with briers;
> Scars to move laughter only.

And the fresh tribute to his soldiership stirs him, despite Cominius' caution, to reopen the quarrel:

> What is the matter
> That being passed for Consul with full voice,
> I am so dishonoured that the very hour
> You take it off again?

—then he sees his error, and checks himself. But, if the Tribunes have failed so far to 'put him to choler', they will not now:

> We charge you, that you have contrived to take
> From Rome all seasoned office, and to wind
> Yourself into a power tyrannical;
> For which you are a traitor to the people.

A two-edged thrust!

> The fires i' the lowest hell fold in the people!
> Call me *their* traitor! . . .

—no holding him after that!

The people are ahead of their leaders here. Spontaneously the cry rises:

> To the rock, to the rock with him!

So now the supple demagogue can play the moderate man, gain credit with the moderate men of the other side, and insure himself against reaction, should that come. The people are right. Marcius' treachery to them

> Deserves the extremest death. . . .
>   But since he hath
> Served well for Rome—

(Brutus is more than a little patronizing) sentence on him shall mercifully be commuted to banishment for life. Neither Menenius' comically frantic

> Is this the promise that you made your mother?

nor Cominius' noble plea, can turn Coriolanus from his defiant wrath, the Tribunes from their triumph. And in their lessoned unison the people echo once and again:

> It shall be so! It shall be so!
> Let him away!
> He's banished, and it shall be so.

Against such a chorus the single voice sounds nobly:

> You common cry of curs! whose breath I hate
> As reek o' the rotten fens, whose love I prize
> As the dead carcasses of unburied men
> That do corrupt my air . . .

and the superlative pride is warranted of the

> I banish you.

To his grim presage of what must be in store for such
a mob and for their Rome the Tribunes listen in com-
placent silence, the people heedlessly, awaiting but the
sight of his departure—

> Despising,
> For you, the city, thus I turn my back:
> There is a world elsewhere.[39]

—to take their time once more from the fugleman-Aedile
with a jubilant

> Our enemy is banished! He is gone! Hoo! hoo!

though its ending is mere wolfish clamour.

'Despising, for you, the city . . .'; there is the first faint
sound—if the actor can accent it, and we are quick to
hear—of the deeper and more tragic discord to come.

Brutus and Sicinius meanwhile will lose nothing of a
popular triumph, nor of their revenge. The hero,
cheered but a few hours since, shall now be hooted
through those same streets:

> Go, see him out at gates, and follow him,
> As he hath followed you, with all despite;
> Give him deserved vexation. . . .

—it is the mob's part. For the assertion of their own
inflated dignity:

> Let a guard
> Attend us through the city.

THE DEPARTURE

Marcius is at once more likable in adversity than in
triumph. Of the cheering crowds that greeted, so short

a while back, his conqueror's entry, of the gathered
Senate praising and honouring him, out of all Rome
nothing friendly seems left him as he takes his way to
exile, but his mother, his wife, two tried friends, and this
silent, useless handful of the young nobility, reluctant
though they are to see their hero depart; and these he
will leave behind. But he makes no complaint, has no
word against the Tribunes—in that omission the perfec-
test contempt!—and, for the people, only the humorously
bitter

> the beast
> With many heads butts me away.

He can rally his mother's spirits by retorting on her a
choice few of the precepts with which she was wont to
load him, and with a bantering

> What, what, what!

when anger breaks from her—

> Now the red pestilence strike all trades in Rome
> And occupations perish!

even as his own, to her reproving, was so apt to do. His
harsher

> Nay, I prithee, woman!

vented upon his wife, is rather curb to himself lest he
give way to grief as she is doing. Menenius—

> Thou old and true Menenius...

—already in tears, he comforts with kindly affection.
Cominius, of sterner mettle, he calls on to

> tell these sad women
> 'Tis fond to wail inevitable strokes
> As 'tis to laugh at them.

To the wreck of his own fortunes there is no more reference than the boyishly simple

> I'll do well yet.

But this is the Marcius passingly glimpsed, who remembered, amid the acclaiming shouts, the poor man in Corioles who had once used him kindly, and, after victory, the widows there, and the 'mothers that lack sons'.

But beneath the cheerful courage, the buoyancy of

> I shall be loved when I am lacked.

we become conscious of a dark, of a sinister sorrow, its shadow apparent in the

> I go alone,
> Like to a lonely dragon, that his fen
> Makes feared and talked of more than seen. . . .

of a suffering repressed, but up-welling in that single

> O, the gods!

He will go to his exile alone, as befits his pride; and whatever they hear of him it shall be

> never of me aught
> But what is like me formerly.

No regrets, therefore, no compunction! He is the same Marcius still; and what cannot soften will but harden him the more.[40]

THOSE LEFT BEHIND

Brutus and Sicinius follow at his heels, the Aedile attending them. Their amiable plan to have a mob hoot him 'out at gates' is thwarted. He has gone. The sooner, therefore, their violence having served its turn, the people are quieted and sent home the better. This is the Aedile's task. Besides, a change of policy is called for now.

> The nobility are vexed. . . .

—and doubtless will repent their weakness in letting Coriolanus go.[41] Therefore, says the sagacious Brutus,

> Now we have shown our power
> Let us seem humbler after it is done
> Than when it was a-doing.

Neither do they fancy an encounter with Volumnia as she now returns—a lowering thundercloud!—with Virgilia and Menenius from the farewell at the gate. But they dodge unavailingly. For the cruel strain of that parting asks fuller relief than in tears—and here they are, very much to the purpose.

Marcius has gone, ominously self-controlled, to nurse his wrongs and breed them into—we shall see what monstrous shape. With Menenius what's done is done. Why waste more words on the fellows? So he finds himself pleading to Volumnia—and as fruitlessly as to her son. For the touch of the unexpected with which Shakespeare is wont to reinforce such eddies in the action as this: Virgilia too, foregoing her 'gracious silence', sets about Sicinius, seconds Volumnia valiantly. The wretched Tribunes take refuge from the volleying words, at first in scandalized astonishment:

> Are you mankind? . . . O blessed heavens!

then in cant; their answer to Volumnia's

> I would my son
> Were in Arabia, and thy tribe before him,
> His good sword in his hand.

to Virgilia's

> He 'ld make an end of thy posterity.

to Volumnia's

> Bastards and all!
> Good man, the wounds that he does bear for Rome

a smooth, white-of-the-eye,

> I would he had continued to his country
> As he began, and not unknit himself
> The noble knot he made.
>> I would he had.

To which her retort comes plumply:

> 'I would he had!' 'Twas you incensed the rabble:
> Cats . . .

Only a dignified departure is left them:

> Pray, let us go.

appropriately tinged with malice:

> Why stay we to be baited
> With one that wants her wits?

They gone, and the storm past, he trusts, Menenius essays for solace:

> You have told them home;
> And, by my troth, you have cause. You'll sup with me?

—old age's comfort in the commonplace! Virgilia, spent by unwonted wrath, is in tears again. But Volumnia:

> Anger's my meat; I sup upon myself,
> And so shall starve with feeding. Come, let's go:
> Leave this faint puling and lament as I do,
> In anger, Juno-like. . . .

These are the natures—like mother, like son—to be broken, never bent; born to catastrophe.

TRADERS IN THE IGNOBLE

Enter a Roman and a Volsce.

Before we see the noble and heroic fallen, infatuate, into infamy, Marcius, amazingly, a traitor to his country, we are given—for edification!—this marginal passage of cheerful trading in the ignoble. The Roman is a Fifth Column fighter, a Volscian spy, on his way to his masters to tell them that, Coriolanus banished, now is the time for them to take their revenge on Rome. His name, it appears, is Nicanor. He luckily encounters a Volscian comrade, one Adrian, who, being in something the same line of business, has been sent to discover him in Rome. He knows Adrian at once, who does not recognize him in his present guise—or disguise:

> You had more beard when I last saw you. . . .

his quizzical apology. The Roman bringing good news, the couple warm to each other:

> the nobles receive so to heart the banishment of that worthy Coriolanus, that they are in a ripe aptness to take all power from the people, and to pluck from them their Tribunes for ever. . . .

—which is not true, we shall learn later; but no matter, since it is good news, not necessarily the truth, that curries favour for your Nicanors.

> I shall, between this and supper, tell you most strange things from Rome, all tending to the good of their adversaries. . . .

continues this pleasant specimen of them, preening himself on the sensation he will make. Coriolanus banished, Aufidius and his Volscians ready to strike:

> I am joyful to hear of their readiness, and am the man, I think, that shall set them in present action. So, sir, heartily well met, and most glad of your company.

And renegade Roman and Volscian go their way together, arm in arm, and as merry as grigs.

The scene forms a bridge between Coriolanus' departure from Rome and his appearance in Antium, suggests some likely period of time passing between the two. Also it shows us a seamier side to the magnificent and tragic treason he is about to commit. He will at least not draw sordid profit from it, and be merry over it.

ANTIUM

Enter Coriolanus, in mean apparel, disguised and muffled.

From now to its end the tone of the play is changed. Marcius is changed, or rather—since men do not change—he seems no longer himself. The vengeance incarnate he becomes is but an empty simulacrum of himself; 'a kind of nothing', Cominius calls him later. His troubles until now have come upon him because he could not learn to be false to his proudly faulty nature. But he has at least been honestly himself in struggling with them—and with the tricky Tribunes—however faultily. Now, under defeat, his untried soul will abjure the spontaneous loyalty, the faith, that had chiefly made him what he was; and he will be the mere tool of his vengeance, until, abjuring this, he is himself again. Meanwhile the passionate and unstable, temptation-tossed Aufidius will be covertly compassing his destruction.

By such twisted and blind paths is it that the action now proceeds.

Marcius appears alone. It is the first such solitary appearance in the play, and will be the more striking because of that.[42] Till now, too, we have seen him only either in fighting trim or in the panoply of his triumph and his consulship, except for the grotesque interlude of the *gown of humility*; his present *mean apparel* is a grimmer variation of it. Outcast, destitute, unarmed, in this city where—pride bitterly reminds him—discovery could mean death, he is seeking his chief enemy Aufidius.[43] And from a soliloquy—short, and the only one allotted to him—we learn why.

He is here to enlist with the Volscians against Rome. It has come to that with him. Neither now nor later are we told of any process of debate within him, any struggle or yielding to temptation. He simply comments now—coldly, cynically—upon the fact that such spiritual revolutions do occur, from hate to love, and love to hate; and

> So with me:
> My birth-place hate I, and my love's upon
> This enemy town.[44]

But it is of a piece with the rest of him that there should have been no such debate or struggle. Of the faculty of introspection he most certainly has none. Not once do we hear him question himself. He acts upon conviction, and is never less than fully convinced. That has helped to make him a fine fighter. Moreover, he must act; inaction is against nature with him, and exile has condemned him to it. And in what he does there will be no compromise, no middle course taken. His soldier's genius and his love of country have inspired him to the doing of great deeds, and the thwarting of these forces in him deprives him of all purpose in life. It is no argument that has turned him traitor. But the present sight of him—so altered and worn that Aufidius, who has five times fought him foot to foot, does not know him—speaks eloquently enough of the lonely misery endured, until, in some dark moment, natural love dead in him, he sought salvation in hate.

Of this sight of him so altered Shakespeare makes much. Deferential enquiry for 'great Aufidius'' house takes him to its hall-fire, to stand there, a gaunt, muffled, forbidding figure, while, contrastingly, cheerful music plays within and the liveried servants pass to and fro on the business of the feast. Ironically submissive to his first rebuff,

> I have deserved no better entertainment,
> In being Coriolanus.

it is the old Marcius that answers with an ominous

> Away!

to the temerity of the Second Servant coming to oust him. What to make of him and that humbly dignified

> Let me but stand; I will not hurt your hearth.

A third servant, with the first two to back him, will deal with the fellow:

> What are you?
> A gentleman.
> A marvellous poor one!
> True, so I am.

But another rash move to oust him brings the Third Servant within reach of that formidable arm, to be sent spinning by a touch from it. These are matters for their master. But awaiting Aufidius, the Third Servant holds his jack-in-office course:

> Where dwell'st thou?
> Under the canopy.
> Under the canopy?
> Ay.
> Where's that?
> I' the city of kites and crows.

while Marcius, the fateful moment nearing, finds a sardonically trivial satisfaction in mystifying these blockheads, a solider one when, turning on the unlucky Third Servant with a

> Thou prat'st; serve with thy trencher: hence!

he whacks him over the head with it.

Aufidius appears; he also, in his feasting finery, little like the man we saw last, bloody with his wounds, savagely sullen in defeat. Genial, flushed with wine, he surveys the uncouth stranger. He has drunk enough to allow for an obstinate repeating of

> What's thy name?

a petulantly wilful

> I know thee not.

while the haggard gaze is levelled at him. And when at last the steeled voice says,

> My name is Caius Marcius....

he sobers to very dumbness, listens at first stupent. Nor is Marcius, nor are we, to know until the whole tale has been rigorously told, how he will take it, what he will do.

Marcius is as absolute as ever, and as proud, still prouder in ill fortune than in good. He does not excuse, nor condescend to justify, nor find fine phrases for what he is ready to do; 'in mere spite' to fight against his 'thankless country', his

> cankered country, with the spleen
> Of all the under fiends . . .

and with as fierce a hate for the 'dastard nobles', his own party, who have suffered him

> by the voice of slaves to be
> Hooped out of Rome.

as for the slaves themselves.

He stoops to no flattery of Aufidius, pretends to no more thought for him and his Volscians than as mere instruments of revenge. A callous bargain; scornfully provokes Aufidius if he will not strike it:

> if so be
> Thou dar'st not this, and that to prove more fortunes
> Thou'rt tired, then, in a word, I also am
> Longer to live most weary, and present
> My throat to thee and to thy ancient malice,
> Which not to cut would show thee but a fool. . . .

Not in mercy then, but as callously, and to his own profit and content, let Aufidius end an enemy's misery here and now. This, in Marcius, is no bravado, but a sober measuring of the worth of revenge to him. He clinches his argument—

> Since I have ever followed thee with hate,
> Drawn tons of blood out of thy country's breast,
> And cannot live but to thy shame, unless
> It be to do thee service.

—and awaits, as uncertain as are we, the issue.

Aufidius, come to credit eyes and ears, has heard dumbfounded these amazing things unfolding, while

within him one responsive impulse ousts another; until
at last:

> O, Marcius, Marcius!
> Each word thou hast spoke hath weeded from my heart
> A root of ancient envy....

—the generous emotion gushes forth, playing like a
warm stream upon the ice, this ice that is Marcius. But
he, for his part, yields, nevertheless, with little grace to
the rhapsodies and embraces of his so suddenly con-
verted foe, nor responds at all to such flowery rhetoric
as the

> Know thou first,
> I loved the maid I married; never man
> Sighed truer breath; but that I see thee here,
> Thou noble thing, more dances my rapt heart
> Than when I first my wedded mistress saw
> Bestride my threshold. Why, thou Mars! ...

Only when he hears of the 'power on foot', of the
Volscian plan already made for

> pouring war
> Into the bowels of ungrateful Rome...

does he tardily, sternly, utter that

> You bless me, gods!

—and the thankfulness must sound strange in his own
ears. For the rest: the leadership proffered, the welcome
from the 'friendly Senators' awaiting him, Aufidius'
superlative

> A thousand welcomes!
> And more a friend than e'er an enemy...

—he accepts it all in silence, passing in to the feast, little like a man so lavishly granted his desire. He goes—already—as to his doom.[45]

Withdrawn to a respectful distance, First and Second Servant have been listening prick-eared:

> Here's a strange alteration!

—and readily do they adapt their artlessly servile minds to it. A great man; they might have known that, of course, despite his rags, from his high-minded way with them. And if great, if, in the next breath 'the rarest man i' the world', why, another must be the lesser. Promptly begins the comically pitiful little shuffle of loyalties, their servile version of the tragic treason upon which they have been eavesdropping.

> a greater soldier than he, you wot on.
> Who? my master?
> Nay, it's no matter for that.
> Worth six on him? Nay, not so neither: but I take him to be the better soldier.
> Faith, look you, one cannot tell how to say that. . . .

—for in prudence we must both commit ourselves, or neither. And to Third Servant strutting excitedly in—happy to have been knocked over the pate with his own trencher by so great a man—and to his reckless

> here's he that was wont to thwack our general. . . .

First Servant makes shocked protest:

> Why do you say 'thwack our general'?

reducing him to double-quick recanting:

> I do not say 'thwack our general. . . . '

But, with a wink and a wag of the head from Second Servant,

Come, we are fellows and friends. . . .

the three are in a tale together.

The consummation of Coriolanus' welcome, the sight of him

> set at upper end o' the table; no question asked him by any of the Senators, but they stand bald before him. . . .

while

> Our general himself makes a mistress of him; sanctifies himself with's hand, and turns up the white o' the eye to his discourse. . . .

—this we see through the simpleton eyes of Third Servant, puffed with the pride of coming fresh from the very sight of it. The comic colouring of the picture heightens, by irony of contrast, its tragic import. The blundering parroting of the talk at table over the noble renegade's prospects—

> for, look you, sir, he has as many friends as enemies; which friends, sir, as it were, durst not, look you, sir, show themselves, as we term it, his friends, whilst he's in directitude. . . . But when they shall see, sir, his crest up again, and the man in blood, they will out of their burrows like conies after rain, and revel all with him.

—embellishes its cynical shrewdness. And already, while Aufidius is still erecting his fragile fane of devotion to his late enemy, this belittling of him by these faithful followers is providing for its wreck.

The scene ends with a noncombatants' chorus in praise of war, coming from Volscians too, who have just been soundly beaten and accorded by their conquerors a merciful peace.

ROME ONCE MORE

The Tribunes Sicinius and Brutus reappear; we are in
Rome again. They are pluming themselves upon

> the present peace
> And quietness o' the people . . .

upon—at this most appropriate moment!—having heard
no more of Coriolanus, while

> Here do we make his friends
> Blush that the world goes well, who rather had,
> Though they themselves did suffer by 't, behold
> Dissentious numbers pestering streets than see
> Our tradesmen singing in their shops and going
> About their functions friendly.

It may be so. But there are men—politicians and
others—who learn, whether by experience or from the
book of their own natures, to think the worst of
everyone. Menenius, passing by, outfaces their complacency—

> Your Coriolanus is not much missed
> But with his friends: the Commonwealth doth stand.
> And so would do, were he more angry at it.

—with a glum, blunt

> All's well, and might have been much better if
> He could have temporised.

After which they take the opportunity that offers of
edifyingly patronizing a group of humbly grateful
citizens—who beseech the gods preserve them, who for

> Ourselves, our wives and children, on our knees,
> Are bound to pray for you both.

to be unctuously repaid by a showering of

> Good den our neighbours.
> Good den to you all, good den to you all....
> Live and thrive!
> Farewell, kind neighbours....

with—a sting for Menenius!—a

> we wished Coriolanus
> Had loved you as we did.

It is for a beginning to the play's ending that we are given this passage of sharp contrast with its beginning; the genial bullying of the citizens by Menenius, their brutal rating by Marcius, here replaced by the soft smiles of their Tribunes—from which official fool's paradise they are very quickly to be expelled.

From its beginning to the moment of Marcius' banishment the play has abounded in physical action, in battles and rioting. From now to the verge of its concluding catastrophe we shall have only the increasing tension of the threat of his reprisals; then, suddenly, their frustration. The battle to be fought now is one of moral forces, culminating in the struggle between Marcius and Volumnia, in which, silently at the last, he accepts defeat. The two sections of the play stand in nearly every respect contrasted. The scene with Aufidius in Antium may be called a bridge between the two; that of Marcius' death is in the nature of an epilogue.

The drama of Coriolanus' approach to his revenge begins at a very zero point, that of Brutus' fatuous

> Rome
> Sits safe and still without him.

Promptly an Aedile appears, to convey, with due official

dignity, the news, brought by 'a slave, whom we have put in prison . . .' that

> the Volsces with two several powers
> Are entered in the Roman territories. . . .

For Menenius, it is Marcius' banishing that has brought them, Aufidius, doubtless, at their head. For Brutus, such an unpleasant thing simply 'cannot be' and the slave must be whipped for saying so. 'Cannot?'; but it has been, thrice within Menenius' memory. Sicinius is as blandly confident:

> Tell not me;
> I know this cannot be.

Whereupon

Enter a Messenger.

Shakespeare gives a hundred lines more to the completing of this scene of the Tribunes' discomfiture, and the whole is a minor masterpiece of treatment. He employs the economical convention of the Messenger, which gives drama the continuity of narrative. But, to vary and enrich it, the story to be told is put into four mouths instead of one, differing in temper and quality, each supplementing or revising the other. The Aedile is unhurried and correct. He has taken order with the slave; he reports the matter; his duty is done. The first Messenger is precipitate and perturbed; wide-eyed. Is it to be believed, this rumour

> that Marcius,
> Joined with Aufidius, leads a power 'gainst Rome,
> And vows revenge . . .

Menenius, for a moment, is at one with the Tribunes in disbelief. But the pendulum is swung violently back by the coming of a second Messenger in all haste to summon the pair without ceremony to the Senate, the ill news cumulated into worse:

> A fearful army, led by Caius Marcius,
> Associated with Aufidius, rages
> Upon our territories; and have already
> O'erborne their way, consumed with fire, and took
> What lay before them.

And, before they can take breath to protest, comes finally Cominius, not only to confirm it but, with grimly humorous satisfaction, to point them out as the culprits:

> O, you have made good work.

Trouble not to be mended by the whipping of a slave! The Tribunes are struck dumb.

Cominius does not spare them, keeps Menenius impatiently demanding his news while he loads them with terrors:

> You have holp to ravish your own daughters, and
> To melt the city leads upon your pates,
> To see your wives dishonoured to your noses—

and—this is the fruit of their rule in Rome—

> *Your* temples burned in their cement, and
> *Your* franchises, whereon you stood . . .

Menenius—his still incredulous

> If Marcius should be joined with Volscians—

extinguished by the sardonic acclaim of

> If!
> He is their god; he leads them like a thing
> Made by some other deity than Nature,

> That shapes man better; and they follow him
> Against us brats. . . .

—takes up the refrain too:

> You have made good work,
> You, and your apron men . . .
> You have made fair work!

until Brutus at last finds a meek and fearful tongue:

> But is this true, sir?

Satisfaction with the vengeance to fall on the Tribunes—capable themselves now of little but agonized grimaces—mingles in Cominius and Menenius with genuine alarm for Rome.[46] This is shot through with renewed pride in Marcius—one of themselves—and the power of his name, this again with the shameful memory that they, his friends, abandoned him.

> We loved him; but, like beasts
> And cowardly nobles, gave way unto your clusters,
> Who did hoot him out o' the city.

The theme of betrayal and self-betrayal permeates the play.

Some 'clusters' gathering round—

> *Enter a troop of Citizens.*

—Menenius can relieve his mind with a little of his old frank abuse of them. Echoing from past clashes,

> Now he's coming. . . .
> as many coxcombs
> As you threw caps up will he tumble down,
> And pay you for your voices. . . .

Cominius echoing him with a

> Ye're goodly things, you voices!

they leave the poor citizens to their pitiful excuses—

> That we did we did for the best; and though we willingly
> consented to his banishment, yet it was against our will.

—and the Tribunes, freed from their daunting presence,
to the flattering futility of

> Go, masters, get you home, be not dismayed:
> These are a side that would be glad to have
> This true which they so seem to fear....

Spiritless all, they go their several ways. Menenius and
Cominius:

> > Shall's to the Capitol?
> O, ay; what else!

The Second Citizen to the rest:

> But come, let's home.

Sicinius to his fellow:

> Pray, let's go.

While as to Brutus, his rueful

> > Would half my wealth
> Would buy this for a lie!

reminds us, incidentally, that politics and the leadership
of the poor can be made to pay.

AUFIDIUS DISILLUSIONED;
MARCIUS SCANNED

The scene between Aufidius and his Lieutenant prepares the play's final stroke without discounting this by

telling us too clearly what it is to be. The impulsive generosity to a fallen enemy has soon burned out in him, and Aufidius, recovered from the experience and ready to treat Marcius as an enemy again, can estimate his virtues and failings the more fairly, even though he is now but the more set to 'potch' at his prodigious rival by

> some way
> Or wrath or craft may get him

For generosity repented has hardened him.

> I do not know what witchcraft's in him. . . .

says the Lieutenant. Well, Aufidius himself has been its victim, and, beside him, will doubtless be

> darkened in this action . . .

—which, however, since there's to be Volscian profit in it, must be carried through. It is only too true that

> All places yield to him ere he sits down;
> And the nobility of Rome are his;
> The Senators and Patricians love him too:
> The Tribunes are no soldiers, and their people
> Will be as rash in the repeal as hasty
> To expel him thence. I think he'll be to Rome
> As is the osprey to the fish, who takes it
> By sovereignty of nature. . . .

But—! Now follows the coldly, carefully, qualified verdict of second-rate success upon first-rate failure:

> First he was
> A noble servant to them, but he could not
> Carry his honours even. Whether 'twas pride . . .
> whether defect of judgment . . .

                    or whether nature,
Not to be other than one thing...
                    but one of these,
As he has spices of them all—not all,
For I dare so far free him—made him feared,
So hated, and so banished....

Let the greatly gifted man remember, then, that

                So our virtues
        Lie in the interpretation of the time....

and, their turn served, are apt to be cancelled out. It
will be so with Coriolanus:

One fire drives out one fire; one nail, one nail;
Rights by rights founder, strengths by strengths do fail.

Aufidius, nursing his plans, his last lethal stroke conceived, is oracular:

            When, Caius, Rome is thine,
    Thou are poor'st of all; then shortly are thou mine.[47]

The scene allows incidentally for the time taken by
Cominius' intercessory visit to Coriolanus, now en-
camped before Rome. This is over when the next opens,
with the tension notably increased by its failure.

NEMESIS NEARS

Enter Menenius, Cominius, Sicinius, Brutus, the two Tribunes,
with others.

—*with others*, listeners and onlookers; a token of the
general anxiety.

Grave as they saw it to be, their enjoyment in saddling
the Tribunes with the blame for it was some sign that
Cominius and Menenius had not, despite all, thought

the situation quite hopeless, had underlyingly felt, rather, that even though they had deserved Marcius' hate, 'and therein showed like enemies', yet they were the men to redeem it. But Cominius has been on his mission since: and

> He would not seem to know me.

Once, indeed, he did call him by his name. But thereafter,

> Coriolanus
> He would not answer to, forbad all names;
> He was a kind of nothing, titleless,
> Till he had forged himself a name o' the fire
> Of burning Rome.

Plea following plea, none moved him, nor will; Cominius is hopelessly sure of it.

Menenius, on the other hand, protesting that he never can succeed if Cominius has failed—

> He called me father,
> But what o' that? ...
> Nay, if he coyed
> To hear Cominius speak, I'll keep at home.

—is plainly 'coying' himself, and only waiting to be pressed harder to consent, in his turn, to go. He is cheerful enough still to be mockingly reminding the now quite crestfallen Brutus and Sicinius that they

> have made good work!
> A pair of Tribunes that have racked for Rome,
> To make coals cheap ...

There is no spirit left in them. Sicinius, begging him to go, is reduced to the pitiful

> if you refuse your aid
> In this so never-needed help, yet do not
> Upbraid's with our distress. . . .

An 'instant army' will be all they can muster for Rome's protection.[48] They fall to wheedling and flattering him. Even if he fails, Sicinius says:

> Yet your good will
> Must have that thanks from Rome, after the measure
> As you intended well.

—which puts him on his mettle. A final show of diffidence, for tribute to 'good Cominius' and his failure, and he is the buoyant old Menenius still:

> He was not taken well; he had not dined.
> The veins unfilled, our blood is cold, and then
> We pout upon the morning, are unapt
> To give or to forgive; but when we have stuffed
> These pipes and these conveyances of our blood
> With wine and feeding, we have suppler souls
> Than in our priest-like fasts. . . .

—the imagery characteristically recalls our first hearing from him with the fable of the Belly and the Members—

> therefore I'll watch him
> Till he be dieted to my request,
> And then I'll set upon him.

And, cheerily confident, off he goes.

Cominius has listened in silence. He shakes his head, strikes the stern note again:

> He'll never hear him. . . .
> I tell you, he does sit in gold, his eye
> Red as 't would burn Rome, and his injury
> The gaoler to his pity. . . .

pictures and prepares us for the pitiless figure we are soon to see.

Then, to end the scene, the step beyond the next is forecast:

> So that all hope is vain,
> Unless his noble mother and his wife,
> Who, as I hear, mean to solicit him
> For mercy to his country....

As the crisis nears the action is knit the closer, that our attention may be the more closely held.

MENENIUS TRIES, AND FAILS

Enter Menenius to the Watch or Guard.

Yet another encounter between patrician and commoners, and a scene of ebb and flow of emotion and humour before—it will be a contrast—the powerfully sustained tension of the trial to come.

Menenius deploys his tact. He answers the sentry's sharp challenge with affable praise:

> You guard like men, 'tis well....

asserts his own quality with accustomed ease:

> but, by your leave,
> I am an officer of state, and come
> To speak with Coriolanus.

—in vain. The sentries disappointingly deserve his praise.

> You may not pass, you must return....
> You'll see your Rome embraced with fire before
> You'll speak with Coriolanus.

He tries the flattery of familiarity:

> Good my friends,
> If you have heard your general talk of Rome,
> And of his friends there, it is lots to blanks,
> My name hath touched your ears: it is Menenius.

is brought to vaunting his own with the great man—

> I tell thee, fellow,
> Thy general is my lover. . . .

—and, in euphemistic phrase, the unconscionable services he has done him:

> Therefore, fellow,
> I must have leave to pass.

Hectorings and wittiness alike get plain answer:

> Faith, sir, if you had told as many lies in his behalf as
> you have uttered words in your own, you should not pass
> here. . . .

But the old gentleman persists, to be given finally a sound and most disrespectful talking to:

> You are a Roman, are you?
> I am, as thy general is.

> Then you should hate Rome, as he does. Can you,
> when you have pushed out your gates the very defender of
> them . . . ?

Truly these Volscian sentries know their own minds and can speak them; the dose no pleasanter to Menenius for its likeness to his own recent medicining of the Tribunes. And if it is to come to an issue between fretful dignity on one side and discipline with cold steel to warrant it on the other—

Sirrah, if thy captain knew I were here, he would use me with estimation.

Come, my captain knows you not.

I mean thy general.

My general cares not for you. Back, I say, go: lest I let forth your half-pint of blood. Back; that's the utmost of your having: back.

Nay, but fellow, fellow—!

At which moment Coriolanus and Aufidius pass.

After a sharp, soldierly

What's the matter?

Coriolanus waits in silence, fulfilment of Cominius' picture of him. Menenius, tossed between emotions, lets the lightest first possess him; tit-for-tat with impudent sentries will restore him his confident good humour.

Now, you companion ... you shall perceive that a Jack guardant cannot office me from my son Coriolanus. ...

He is himself again in the jaunty extravagance of

guess but by my entertainment with him, if thou standest not i' the state of hanging, or of some death more long in spectatorship, and crueller in suffering; behold now presently and swoon for what's to come upon thee.

It gives him time, too, in which to face this changed Marcius, distant, mute, hostile, companioned there with Aufidius. But he neither hesitates nor calculates. Eloquence overflows in affection and tears:

The glorious gods sit in hourly synod about thy particular prosperity, and love thee no worse than thy old father Menenius does! O my son! my son! thou art preparing fire for us: look thee, here's water to quench it. ...

and, for a final fillip, into the familiar humour:

> The good gods assuage thy wrath, and turn the dregs of
> it upon this varlet here; this, who, like a block, hath denied
> my access to thee.

The one word of the answer, spanning the space between
them—

> Away!

—falls like a blow. The old man staggers under it. Had
he ears for aught else he might note in the sequent

> Wife, mother, child, I know not. . . .

the flaw in the armour of which that too rigid figure is
himself aware, might even read in the strain of the

> Yet—for I loved thee—
> Take this along, I writ it for thy sake
> And would have sent it. . . .

in this letter with which he is dismissed, defence ready
to crumble. But pride, if not affection, is now too
wounded for him to think of aught else.
Coriolanus and Aufidius pass on their way:

> This man, Aufidius,
> Was my beloved in Rome; yet thou beholdst

to which utterance of twisted, tortured pride Aufidius
pays sardonic tribute:

> You keep a constant temper.

But Menenius can take a blow gallantly still, and pay
back mockery with mockery. To the sentries' jubilant

> Now, sir, is your name Menenius?

'Tis a spell, you see, of much power. You know the way
home again.

Do you hear how we are shent for keeping your greatness
back?

What cause, do you think, I have to swoon?

he returns as good as he gets, and better:

I neither care for the world, nor your general: for such
things as you, I can scarce think there's any, y'are so
slight. . . .

—but it is graver defiance than that—

He that hath a will to die by himself, fears it not from
another. Let your general do his worst. . . .

—no business of theirs though!

For you, be that you are, long; and your misery increase
with age! I say to you, as I was said to, Away!

They are left laughing; won, nevertheless, to the verdict
of

A noble fellow, I warrant him.

VOLUMNIA COMES, AND THE CONQUEROR
IS CONQUERED

Coriolanus and Aufidius were, it seems, on their way
to a council of war; they are taking their places at its
table now.[49] First, formally and for all to hear, the two
exchange assurances that so far in this strange business
all has been frankly done. Aufidius is most generous in
his assurance. Coriolanus then falls to confession; and—
how changed!—it is of kindly, politic trickery. 'With a
cracked heart' it was, then, that he stood outfacing

Menenius there; and he had offered him in the letter, to make things easier for them both, something to carry away that he yet knew must be rejected. It was only

> A very little
> I have yielded to. . . .

but it is right they know it. That is all finished now. Then

> *Shout within.*

He asks what it may mean, knowing too well:

> Shall I be tempted to infringe my vow
> In the same time 'tis made? . . .

The dreaded trial has come. He steels himself:

> I will not.

The pending struggle has been fully prepared. Cominius, Consul and General, revered as both, kneeling, repulsed, the loved Menenius dismissed—this the one aspect, completed by the sentry's admiring view of the traitor-hero as

> the rock, the oak not to be wind-shaken.

For another; he has armoured himself with an oath offered to Aufidius, a vow solemnly taken. The closer our sight of him, the plainer it is that nevertheless he feels not so sure of the issue. He has a fight still to win. And the play is not over yet.

When he sees the figures of the women approaching the scene's tension rises instantly to high pitch. It is to be a long scene, of a struggle the deadlier for its quiet; even as wrestlers in a lock strain silently, motionless, until one is exhausted and as silently loosens grasp, and the match is over. The tension will hardly relax; a moment's

relief, and it tightens again. The action is clearly articu-
lated, deliberate, sparse; the speech indicates it and
allows for it. Marcius is its firm and sensitive centre. The
argument ranges round him, widely, closely; touches him
as husband, lover, father, son, Roman, uses his wife's
tears, his boy's gallantly shrill defiance, Volumnia's desperate barring of the end to this road on which—it was
she that set him. Silence is his ultimate answer; and the
whole, with its passion, in its intimacies and simplicities,
is keyed to the tenor of a great event.

Note the dramatic generalship with which Shakespeare
employs his forces. First is the duel effect made by the
mute, anonymous approach of the women, their speech,
even for a moment their identity, held in reserve, while
Marcius, describing them, at once interprets besides the
effect made on him.[50] The battle begins and ends with
a struggle within himself. It will end in silence; it begins
articulately. Back and forth he is swayed; by the very
sight, the first since his exile, of those three that he
loves.[51]

> But out, affection!
> All bond and privilege of nature break!
> Let it be virtuous to be obstinate! . . .

Then, his wife's 'doves' eyes' turned on him:

> I melt, and am not
> Of stronger earth than others. . . .

Lastly, to break the spell of Volumnia's grave obeisance,
and against his boy's

> aspect of intercession, which
> Great nature cries, 'Deny not.' . . .

he violently flings away with

> Let the Volsces
> Plough Rome and harrow Italy; I'll never
> Be such a gosling to obey instinct, but stand
> As if a man were author of himself
> And knew no other kin.

But he is drawn to face Virgilia and her gentle

> My lord and husband.

to invite, with his repelling

> These eyes are not the same I wore in Rome.

her as gently keen

> The sorrow that delivers us thus changed
> Makes you think so.

He owns to the effect of the thrust:

> Like a dull actor now,
> I have forgot my part, and I am out,
> Even to a full disgrace....

and, the next instant, she is in his arms.

> Best of my flesh,
> Forgive my tyranny; but do not say
> For that 'Forgive our Romans.' O, a kiss,
> Long as my exile, sweet as my revenge!
> Now, by the jealous queen of heaven, that kiss
> I carried from thee, dear, and my true lip
> Hath virgined it e'er since. You gods! I prate....

Much of Marcius is lit up in this. In his love for his wife
a quality of nature rarer than that bred of the exchange
of pride between him and his mother. From it had
sprung at his triumphal entry into Rome the thought of
the Volscian widows left desolate; the kindling touch of

her lips might free him to sudden forgiveness now. Love
and hate are near akin in him, are but the two sides of
the one shield; and each he justifies by what he does,
and that by what he is. To spend more words on either
is to 'prate'.

He turns to

> the most noble mother of the world . . .

and with a

> Sink, my knee, i' the earth. . . .

gives her full due. She bids him

> stand up blest!

then kneels herself, thus 'unproperly', she says, to

> Show duty, as mistaken all this while,
> Between the child and parent.

She shocks him, and means to. But the irony is rather
in the event; and when he raises her she unconsciously
gives it voice again:

> Thou art my warrior;
> I holp to frame thee.

She did indeed! As well her teaching as his learning has
brought them to this pass.[52]

Valeria, dignified, beautiful, silent—

> The noble sister of Publicola,
> The moon of Rome, chaste as the icicle
> That's curded by the frost from purest snow,
> And hangs on Dian's temple . . .

—follows in her place. Is she also to find her fate in the
sack of a city?[53] Lastly the boy is put forward, sturdily

stubborn, even against this great man his father's thrilling exhortation, until Volumnia takes order with a stern

> Your knee, sirrah!

and Marcius, delighting in him:

> That's my brave boy!

He, who has never counted the odds at which he fought, has never had to fight, surely, at such odds as this.

Volumnia, with due dignity, opens her plea. Upon its very threshold he stops her, the more petitionary himself in his denials:

> Do not bid me
> Dismiss my soldiers. . . .
> > tell me not
> Wherein I seem unnatural, desire not
> To allay my rages and revenges. . . .

But she answers with an insistence matching his own:

> O, no more, no more!
> You have said you will not grant us any thing,
> For we have nothing else to ask but that
> Which you deny already. . . .

an obstinacy too:

> Yet we will ask. . . .

So he turns back to Aufidius and the Volsces, returns to their council table, seats himself there again, as in judgment with them.[54]

Her speech before this strange tribunal comes from a Volumnia compelled at last to see Coriolanus' valour from the standpoint of the vanquished. The exulting fierceness of her once-triumphant

Death, that dark spirit, in 's nervy arm doth lie. . . .

has melted to the grief of

> Think with thyself
> How more unfortunate than all living women
> Are we come hither. . . .
> the mother, wife and child to see
> The son, the husband and the father tearing
> His country's bowels out. . . .

grief highly argued:

> thou barr'st us
> Our prayers to the gods. . . .
> for how can we,
> Alas! how can we for our country pray,
> Whereto we are bound, together with thy victory,
> Whereto we are bound? . . .

Yet out of the deadlock and division to which pride and wrath—his fostering of it, and hers—have brought them, out of the fatal dilemma—

> for either thou
> Must, as a foreign recreant, be led
> With manacles through our streets, or else
> Triumphantly tread on thy country's ruin. . . .

—she sees one way. But—Volumnia still!—her passion bids fair to swamp her very plea for following it

> For myself, son . . .
> if I cannot persuade thee
> Rather to show a noble grace to both parts
> Than seek the end of one, thou shalt no sooner
> March to assault thy country than to tread—
> Trust to 't, thou shalt not—on thy mother's womb,
> That brought thee to this world.

Virgilia echoing her with

> Ay, and mine,
> That brought you forth this boy, to keep your name
> Living to time.

even the child, ridiculously, gallantly defiant:

> A' shall not tread on me;
> I'll run away till I am bigger, but then I'll fight.

Thus does this breed set about making peace.[55]

Marcius sits silent until the effect of the triply un-answerable challenge has died away. Then, quietly, re-flectively, to the foiled self in him:

> Not of a woman's tenderness to be,
> Requires nor child nor woman's face to see.

And he rises and moves mechanically away, defeated and avoiding defeat. Volumnia's pursuing arguments sound strange to him; from her to him they well may! 'Our suit is, that you reconcile . . .'! The Volsces are to say,

> 'This mercy we have showed'; the Romans
> 'This we received'; and each in either side
> Give the all-hail to thee, and cry 'Be blest
> For making up this peace!'

She to be telling him:

> The end of war's uncertain. . . .

asking him:

> Thinkst thou it honourable for a noble man
> Still to remember wrongs?

Is this Volumnia?

It is here that his silence comes to be stressed by the baffled recurrence of her

> Speak to me, son. . . .
> Why does not speak? . . .
> yet here he lets me prate
>
> Like one i' the stocks. . . .
>
> He turns away.

And the technique of the scene is in itself remarkable. Usually such a speech as this will concentrate our attention on the speaker; and, the more strongly, the less of even a side-glance from us can surrounding characters claim. But Volumnia makes Virgilia's tears, the child's high spirit, Valeria's quiet dignity a living part of the action, adding their eloquence in its kind to her own, to wield it all against the opposing silence of Marcius' last stand.

His silence counterbalances, and by a little will out-balance, her share in the encounter. For she ceases her attack, unbeaten but munition spent—

> I am husht until our city be a-fire,
> And then I'll speak a little.

—and still he has not answered.

> *Holds her by the hand, silent.*

is the stage direction, Shakespeare's own certainly. In the silence is his answer, and he spares her all other. She has won. And for him

> the heavens do ope,
> The gods look down, and this unnatural scene
> They laugh at. . . .

—unnatural, since pride and her pride in him have brought him to this, and she that helped make him is bidding him remake himself now. And that he can no longer do. Mercy and forgiveness are not for him. And it is she that has vanquished him. Only she could.

He gently warns her of what may follow:

> O, my mother, mother! O!
> You have won a happy victory to Rome;
> But for your son, believe it, O, believe it,
> Most dangerously you have with him prevailed
> If not most mortal to him. . . .

But, the great strain relaxed, she seemingly thinks but of her victory and does not heed. He braces himself again—as at the beginning of the struggle, so now to what must follow—with a

> But let it come.

next, pride abated, turns to Aufidius—out of all the world—for sympathy:

> Now, good Aufidius,
> Were you in my stead, would you have heard
> A mother less, or granted less, Aufidius?

—who, coldly observant, commits himself to no more than a

> I was moved withal.

and then comes to the decision that is to be his death:

> for my part,
> I'll not to Rome. I'll back with you; and pray you,
> Stand to me in this cause. . . .

Aufidius felt sure (we heard him say) that even those in Rome who feared Marcius most

> Will be as rash in the repeal, as hasty
> To expel him thence . . .

But if the traitor prefers conflict in Corioles, so much the worse for him—and the better for Aufidius!

It is not in Marcius to enter Rome again. For the last time—he knows to what he may be going—he lets himself be stirred to his depths:

> O, mother! wife!

After which, lest they should now catch up with his thoughts, should try, as it seems they will, to keep him there, he plays the man of affairs with them, the game loser:

> Ay, by and by;
> But we will drink together, and you shall bear
> A better witness back than words. . . .

Gallantly courteous, he addresses the whole train:

> Ladies, you deserve
> To have a temple built to you: all the swords
> In Italy, and her confederate arms,
> Could not have made this peace.

ROME DELIVERED

Rome fearfully awaits news of her fate. *We* already know it, so the suspense must not be spun out. Menenius returning meets Sicinius, while the issue is still, he supposes, in doubt, and he can avenge on him his own repulse by assurance that Volumnia will do no better. The old Tribune is in despair:

> He loved his mother dearly.

and Menenius finds satisfaction of the perverser sort in:

> So did he me; and he no more remembers his mother now than an eight-year-old horse. The tartness of his face

sours ripe grapes. . . . Mark what mercy his mother shall
bring from him: there is no more mercy in him than there
is milk in a male tiger; that shall our poor city find. . . .

and so falls back upon

> all this is long of you.

There comes yet more for him in a messenger's tidings
that the plebeians have now seized upon the wretched
Brutus,

> And hale him up and down; all swearing, if
> The Roman ladies bring not comfort home,
> They'll give him death by inches.

So when the good news arrives that

> the ladies have prevailed,
> The Volscians are dislodged, and Marcius gone. . . .

he can but be at first a trifle disappointed. Sicinius, for
his part, who would not credit the bad news when it
came, is wary of the good news now.

> Friend,
> Art thou certain this is true? is it most certain?

But the rejoicing sounds without are evidence enough:

> *Trumpets, hoboyes, drums beate altogether.*

Shakespeare's theatre can do no more. From Menenius,
then, breaks a generously happy

> This is good news:
> I will go meet the ladies. This Volumnia
> Is worth of consuls, senators, patricians,
> A city full . . .

with, for a last humorous gibe,

> of Tribunes, such as you,
A sea and land full.

and he is away.[56]
Sicinius, so barely saved, must reassert his dignity:

> First, the gods bless you for your tidings; next,
> Accept *my* thankfulness.

The Messenger, afflicted by no such pomposity:

> Sir, we have all
> Great cause to give great thanks.

Rome's saviours near the city; at point to enter! A Tribune's benign presence is called for:

> We will meet them,
And help the joy.

VOLUMNIA'S TRIUMPH

*Enter two Senators, with Ladies, passing over the stage,
with other Lords.*

Thus this short stretch of the action ends, with such a procession, so acclaimed, as that which once brought Coriolanus back in triumph from his wars. And the people are to

> Unshout the noise that banished Marcius,
> Repeal him with the welcome of his mother. . . .

—but too late.

THE END

Enter Tullus Aufidius with Attendants.

—the *Attendants* an opening suggestion of authority.

Aufidius gives the tone to this, the play's last scene. Its doings are to win him success, and he promptly assumes control of them:

> Go tell the lords o' the city I am here;
> Deliver them this paper: having read it,
> Bid them repair to the market place. . . .
>   Him I accuse
> The city ports by this hath entered, and
> Intends to appear before the people, hoping
> To purge himself with words. Dispatch.

Of all men, Coriolanus, 'to appear before the people' that he may 'purge himself with words'! The attendants go about the business given them, and are replaced by

> 3 or 4 Conspirators of Aufidius' Faction.

and he and they proceed to make the case against Coriolanus.

Aufidius is an injured man, and although

> We must proceed as we do find the people.

—as troublesome in Corioles as in Rome apparently—it should not be hard to show him a wronged man. Such generosity as he has shown, with such advantage taken of it! For the 'witchcraft', we may note, which once made men 'fly to the Roman'—Aufidius among them!—has now become the

>   dews of flattery,
>   Seducing so my friends . . .

And, above all,

> When he had carried Rome, and that we looked
> For no less spoil than glory—

For this, at least, Aufidius promises,

> my sinews shall be stretched upon him. . . .
>   he sold the blood and labour
> Of our great action; therefore he shall die,
> And I'll renew me in his fall. . . .

—at which moment

> *Drums and trumpets sound, with great shouts of the people.*

So Marcius comes in triumph, if not back to Rome,
into Corioles. His rival stands to listen. And, were more
provocation needed, friends provide it in their low reminder that

> Your native town you entered like a post,
> And had no welcomes home; but he returns
> Splitting the air with noise.
>   And patient fools,
> Whose children he hath slain, their base throats tear
> With giving him glory.

The lords of the city, now arriving, offer their welcome, none the less—which Aufidius, with a certain
sulky modesty, disclaims. More to the purpose, they have
digested his charges against Marcius, the last that he
should

>   give away
> The benefit of our levies, answering us
> With our own charge: making a treaty where
> There was a yielding; this admits no excuse.

and Aufidius can afford to stand aside; with an

> He approaches: you shall hear him.

Note now the stage direction:

Enter Coriolanus marching with drum and colours; the Commoners being with him.

He is in full panoply of war, an impressive, a commanding figure. This is he to whose side Aufidius' soldiers flocked. Aufidius himself looks and will feel nothing beside him. Moreover, the commoners are with him, to cheer or hoot him, as the Roman commoners did. They are cheering him now. And whatever the Volscian case against him, he means to make a good one for himself. But it is a hardened Marcius that makes it:

> Hail, lords! I am returned your soldier,
> No more infected with my country's love
> Than when I parted hence, but still subsisting
> Under your great command. . . .

a Marcius brought to claiming that

> Our spoils we have brought home
> Doth more than counterpoise a full third part
> The charges of the action. . . .

—the man of whom it could be said in Rome that

> Our spoils he kicked at,
> And looked upon things precious as they were
> The common muck of the world. . . .

Not that a third of the cost of the war is matter of great account either! But he means to make himself a place here too. He must. He has no other left.

Aufidius sees this, and that he must strike hard, and without delay. 'Traitor' is a sharp blow; and the derisive 'Marcius' added—

> Ay, Marcius, Caius Marcius. Dost thou think
> I'll grace thee with that robbery, thy stolen name
> Coriolanus in Corioles?

—will draw his enemy towards tricky ground. He says no word of his own wrongs; only that:

> You lords and heads o' the state, perfidiously
> He has betrayed your business, and given up,
> For certain drops of salt, your city Rome,
> I say 'your city'. . . .

The commoners are listening too, the conspirators are on the watch. Aufidius drives on:

> Breaking his oath and resolution like
> A twist of rotten silk . . .
> He whined and roared away your victory. . . .

To all of which Coriolanus has reasonable answer. But the insults to his soldiership, his manhood, blot out all else:

> Hear'st thou, Mars?

Aufidius ends with a contemptuous

> Name not the god, thou boy of tears. . . .
> No more.

Marcius, incandescent with anger:

> Measureless liar, thou hast made my heart
> Too great for what contains it. . . .

yet it is the 'boy' that has pricked deepest, and the more intolerably for the truth of it. Of the lies let these 'grave lords' judge; but for the liar himself:

> Who wears my stripes impressed upon him, that
> Must bear my beating to his grave . . .

Here is the old exultant—that boyishly exultant—Marcius. Let his enemies take vengeance on him if they will:

> Cut me to pieces, Volsces; men and lads,
> Stain all your edges on me. . . .

for

> If you have writ your annals true, 'tis there,
> That, like an eagle in a dove-cote, I
> Fluttered your Volscians in Corioles:
> Alone I did it. Boy!

One of Shakespeare's master-moments this, in which he brings the tragic figure to the very edge of the ridiculous, but stays him there.

Even as his friends in Rome were wont to check and save him, so might the Volscian lords, would he but let them:

> The man is noble, and his fame folds in
> This orb o' the earth. His last offence to us
> Shall have judicious hearing. . . .

But Aufidius, who while he rages can still calculate, in appealing to them is appealing over their heads to the commoners, those commoners that, in Corioles as in Rome, Coriolanus will so obligingly provoke for him:

> Why, noble lords,
> Will you be put in mind of his blind fortune,
> Which was your shame, by this unholy braggart,
> 'Fore your own eyes and ears?

It is the conspirators' cue for a fomenting

> Let him die for 't.

and, as once before, the mob howls for his blood. As once before too he draws his sword, disdaining aid:

> O! that I had him,
> With six Aufidiuses, or more, his tribe,
> To use my lawful sword.

An 'Insolent villain!' from Aufidius gives the conspirators

their cue again; and, with vociferous 'Kills' to drown the cries of 'Hold!', they crowd in on him, daggers drawn. He falls, and

> *Aufidius stands on him.*

He stands on him! Could words say more?
His first thought is to justify his deed—

> My noble masters, hear me speak.

—and not until he hears the shocked reproaches does he realize what he is shamefully doing now.

> O, Tullus! . . .
> Tread not upon him. Masters, all be quiet.
> Put up your swords.

But it will not be so difficult to persuade moderate men that, though it has been wrong to kill him, yet Coriolanus is better dead. Therefore

> Bear from hence his body,
> And mourn you for him. Let him be regarded
> As the most noble corse that ever herald
> Did follow to his urn.

The Second Lord already sees clearly the other side of the matter:

> His own impatience
> Takes from Aufidius a great part of blame.
> Let's make the best of it.

and Aufidius adds in all sincerity:

> My rage is gone,
> And I am struck with sorrow.

The Verse

IN listening to the play we shall be conscious of the verse as a thing in itself only at certain intenser moments, which are thus—by one metrical device or another—emphasized and made memorable. For the rest it will impress us rather as powerful, rounded speech, resonant somewhat above the ordinary, and, in particular, borne forward by a most compelling rhythm. A change from verse to prose, even, we may chiefly remark as a change of temper, a lessening of emotional pressure, or merely a timely contrast.

Not for long now—by the measure of his swift development—has Shakespeare habitually dealt in 'set pieces' of verse, 'Queen Mab' speeches, pronouncements that 'All the world's a stage' or that 'The quality of mercy is not strained'; and, even when he did, they would seldom lack some direct dramatic sanction. Portia's, for instance, is legitimate forensic eloquence, and Jaques has been cast, in the Arden pastoral, for the part of moralizer-in-chief to the banished Duke. Again, the speeches of the two Henrys upon sleeplessness, ceremony and kingship may, in method, be more rhetorical than reflective, but they suit both character and occasion. A little later, Brutus' ordered soliloquies come as the due expression of an ordered mind, and Mark Antony's oratory is directed first to his Roman hearers, and only through them upon us, the audience; and let actor or audience forget this and its dramatic purpose is warped. Then, with *Hamlet*—and in Hamlet's own speech particularly—we come within reach of a seeming spontaneity. Shakespeare allows him all possible scope of expression, both in prose and verse; and in the choice between them, and in the form and colour of the verse as well as in its content, his every mood, of contemplation, irony or despair, will be sensitively reflected. It is, of course, only a 'seeming spontaneity'. People do not naturally speak verse, be it but blank verse; and even in prose, and for the simple speech of citizen or peasant, Shakespeare never lapses into an *imitated* spontaneity, so to forfeit all the aids of form and accepted convention.[57]

It is a consonant part—this reaching towards a seeming spontaneity—of Shakespeare's general development as a dramatist, and it necessarily tends to loosen and even break down the form of the verse. To begin with he is a poet writing plays—as Marlowe was, and Lyly—and his lengths of verse, often narrative or descriptive in their bent, will readily fall into regular form. And for long enough the form, a little eased or a little fortified, accommodates the direct expression of character and emotion very well, as, for instance, in the forthright Hotspur, less well for the subtler Richard II. It is when character and emotion gain complexity and extraordinary force that—as a stream in flood eats its banks away—the verse breaks bounds; then Shakespeare himself has developed from the poet writing plays into the true dramatic poet.

This is not a quibbling distinction, it indicates a very fertile difference. Incidentally, it overrides the question of the medium used, prose or verse. *Macbeth* could have been written in prose without fundamental loss; it is poetically conceived. There is as much poetry in the prose of *As You Like It* as in its verse.[58] Convention and convenience, both to the dramatist and his actors, will commonly have recommended verse; but from the beginning Shakespeare seemingly tended to use whichever, that or prose, better suited his immediate purpose.[59] Shylock's supreme outburst is in prose; there is dramatic value in the mere contrast with the mellifluous verse surrounding it. *Richard II*'s exceptional uniformity of verse remains unbroken, though we might look for prose in the short gardeners' scene. Bottom and Weaver and his friends demand prose, if only because they have a play to rehearse and perform. Its medium must not be their own, and it will go best in doggerel. But who that could write verse would not write it for the rest of *A Midsummer Night's Dream?* Prose suits Falstaff to perfection; and Beatrice and Benedick, Rosalind and Orlando, leave the verse of the plays they animate sounding dull by comparison. But, comedy yielding to tragedy, verse comes to its own again; since it can excite emotion and sustain illusion as prose cannot.

The verse must not, in its new-won freedom, be let flow too freely, too slackly, or it will lose its power—as did so much of the verse of Shakespeare's immediate successors; and when Dryden and his school thought at last to come to the rescue the mischief had gone too far. With Shakespeare himself there will always be some recurrent check, in the shape of a line or a passage of stricter metre. Not mechanically inserted; if dramatic demand breaks the form of the verse, dramatic demand will also restore it. Hamlet is recalled from the overflowing emotion of

> Bloody, bawdy villain!
> Remorseless, treacherous, lecherous, kindless villain!
> O, vengeance!

to the controlled thought of

> About my brain! I have heard
> That guilty creatures, sitting at a play,
> Have by the very cunning of the scene ...

And the firm rhythm of Othello's

> Farewell the tranquil mind! farewell content!
> Farewell the plumed troop and the big wars. ...

or of his

> It is the cause, it is the cause, my soul:
> Let me not name it to you, you chaste stars! . . .

—with other such counterbalancings to the succession of minor metrical liberties lodged (inconspicuously for the most part) in the general run of the verse—help to keep him heroically dominant over the commoner traffic of the play. The larger the liberties taken, the greater the need for this recurrent control. For drama is a disciplined art, hedged in by a hundred restrictions. It is akin to poetry and to verse in that, and the restrictions themselves are akin. And in the poetic play a loosening of the ties of verse only leaves it to depend the more upon a more essential order of character and idea, upon which—and not chiefly upon form—it must in fact be built. But this will be essentially poetic and dramatic too since it will deal with the metaphysical things with which poetry most properly deals, and with conflicts of the human will. Shakespeare evolves, then, for the major medium of his maturer plays, this enfranchised verse; a rhythmic and melodious speech, powerful and malleable at once. Of its form we shall often be but indefinitely aware; as much is kept as will keep the structure intact, now more, now less being needed. Little sense of artifice is left to intervene between us and the acted play; the medium grows transparent. Sacrificing none of them, he moulds his diversity of means into a unity of dramatic expression; and he lifts us—we have only to surrender— to the level of it.

Not much is to be gained—in appreciation, that is to say, of its living qualities—by carrying such verse, cold and dead, to the dissecting table, there to demonstrate its spondees and dactyls, its overrun lines and feminine endings. Assuredly Shakespeare never planned it so; and, multiply rules as we may in trying to round his practice

into some sort of system, the exceptions will outrun
them. We do not think in terms of prosody at all of

> I am dying, Egypt, dying; only
> I here importune death awhile, until
> Of many thousand kisses the poor last
> I lay upon thy lips.

noting, as we speak the lines, that the first has—rather
surprisingly—the orthodox ten syllables; nor do we remember Lear's

> Never, never, never, never, never!

as five successive trochees. Form and meaning are not
to be separated.

But for all the freedom in the general run of the verse
the later plays furnish us still with rhymed couplets enough,
'sentences', lengths of octosyllabics, and such like conventional forms. There is the difference, however, that these
things now owe their place to some particular dramatic use
that can be made of them—to clinch an argument, stress
a desperate moment or clarify a reflective one.[60] And the
use is overt; the effect made will stand out like a patch of
bright colour, or, if the main speech-fabric hereabouts is
already brightly coloured, of contrasting shade. Shakespeare never abandons a well-tried dramatic device; let it
still serve his purpose, that is the only test.

One freedom opens up another. Individual expression
besides, the verse may now be moulded to the character
of particular scenes, or of the play itself. The fantastic
rhyming of Edgar and the Fool, attuned to Lear's own
lunacy, does much for the storm-scenes in *King Lear*. The
verse of *Othello* combines energy and colour and ease in
a manner of its own. And contrast in colour and in
rhythm generally is to be added to the others between
Antony and Cleopatra and *Coriolanus*. Imperial Rome and

exotic Egypt and the searching minds and sweeping passions which inform them—the magnificent many-faceted verse of the one reflects these, even as concentration on a narrower strife finds fitting voice in the closer woven, more angular, lines of *Coriolanus*.

There is little in subject or characters to carry Shakespeare off his feet and set the verse of *Coriolanus* soaring. Egoism, rivalry, cunning and pride (the more generous traits, making by comparison a poor show) leave the radiant passages few, incidental usually and as likely as not to illuminate some minor figure.

> Now the fair goddess Fortune
> Fall deep in love with thee: and her great charms
> Misguide thy opposers' swords! Bold gentleman,
> Prosperity be thy page!

—the old warrior, himself outdone, but lavish in admiration of his heroically truculent young comrade; those few lines brighten the whole scene. And it is to an anonymous messenger that is given the brilliant little

> 'Tis thought
> That Marcius shall be Consul.
> I've seen the dumb men throng to see him, and
> The blind to hear him speak: matrons flung gloves,
> Ladies and maids their scarfs and handkerchers,
> Upon him as he passed: the nobles bended
> As to Jove's statue, and the commons made
> A shower and thunder with their caps and shouts:
> I never saw the like.[61]

DRAMATIC VERSE INDEED

The verse in the main is vigorous, and it drives hard and exclusively at its dramatic purpose. The rhythm is apt to be of more import than the melody. The words are often unmusical in themselves, and they may be crushed into the lines like fuel to stoke a furnace. It is a cast of speech well fitting the reason-searching strife which pervades the play; and none in the canon is fuller of quarrel of one sort or another from beginning to end.

But if the verse—with nothing in the matter of it to stir the imagination—does not soar, neither does it ever sag. The play in this respect has not a single weak spot. One detects, in the frequent lack of clarity, a certain effort in the writing; but at least the effort is never shirked. The most patent instance comes, perhaps, in Aufidius' summary of his rival's failings:

> Whether 'twas pride,
> Which out of daily fortune ever taints
> The happy man; whether defect of judgment,
> To fail in the disposing of those chances
> Which he was lord of; or whether nature,
> Not to be other than one thing, not moving
> From th' casque to th' cushion, but commanding peace
> Even with the same austerity and garb
> As he controlled the war; but one of these,
> As he hath spices of them all—not all,
> For I dare so far free him—made him feared,
> So hated and so banished. . . .

—and so on, until the long succession of saving clauses is tied off in a complex aphorism.[62] If Shakespeare could not render down his thought into something clearer than this he might better, surely, have omitted the passage altogether. But no; Aufidius at this point, he feels, needs rationalizing, Coriolanus too. And if the idea involved will not distill and flow freely, it must just be wrung out. It cannot be omitted, and a flaw left in the fabric of thought.

Clarity yields to intensity. Witness Sicinius' malignly prescient

> Doubt not
> The commoners for whom we stand, but they
> Upon their ancient malice will forget
> With the least cause these his new honours; which
> That he will give them, make I as little question
> As he is proud to do't.

Put on paper, the last part of this may not parse well. But in speech, if the speaker be skilful, the thoughts themselves can be related—the 'which' linked to the 'least cause', the 'proud' given its proper prominence— and the very lack of clarity be made to suggest their urgency.

Volumnia's disingenuous arguments, which send Marcius back to the market place, are wound out smoothly:

> If it be honour in your wars to seem
> The same you are not...
>   now it lies on you to speak
> To the people; not by your own instruction,
> Nor by the matter which your heart prompts you,
> But with such words that are but roted in
> Your tongue, though but bastards and syllables
> Of no allowance to your bosom's truth.
> Now this no more dishonours you at all...

—the verse cold, sustained, regular, unmelodious, fitted to the occasion and her temper, its sense aridly clear.

The man himself, if but a worse side of him, is alive both in the matter and manner of Marcius' beginning:

> What's the matter, you dissentious rogues,
> That, rubbing the poor itch of your opinion,
> Make yourselves scabs?

with its curt 'What's the matter?', its veritably physical
repugnance for the 'rogues' set in the ugly images which
follow, these followed the next moment by

> What would you have, you curs,
> That like not peace nor war? The one affrights you,
> The other makes you proud. He that trusts to you,
> When he should find you lions, finds you hares;
> Where foxes, geese: you are no surer, no,
> Than is the coal of fire upon the ice,
> Or hailstone in the sun.

with its banging-about of contraries, like so many boxes
on the ear; the scolding then carried on into the
crowded, contemptuous

> Hang 'em! They say!
> They'll sit by the fire, and presume to know
> What's done i' the Capitol; who's like to rise,
> Who thrives, and who declines; side factions, and give out
> Conjectural marriages. . . .

together with such tunelessness as is in 'hunger broke
stone walls', 'horns o' the moon', 'insurrection's arguing'—suitably, not a line of clear melody or smooth
rhythm.

Further than which—one may at this point note—in
the shaping and attuning of his verse to the expression
of *individual* character, Shakespeare, here or elsewhere,
in this play or another, hardly goes. For there must be
some prevailing unity of form, or a play would fall in
pieces; so, whatever the liberty given to the verse, its
ten-syllable, five-stress foundation is left (as we have seen
already) solidly underlying it still. And characters, even
at their most individual, are still only emergent from
type; this is true of Hamlet, of Falstaff even, Rosalind
or Beatrice. Coriolanus himself is a variation of the

soldier-hero, Aufidius of a villainous rival, while Menenius fills—if overfills—the place of the worldly-wise old counsellor, and Volumnia traces a little less theatrical descent as Roman matron. And the scope and individual character of all dramatic speech, be this remembered, since it must be instantly understood, has its limits there.

Dialogue and action are made to interpret one the other with exact economy. We actually see, first the failure, then the exciting success of the attack on Corioles, the city's capture and its token sacking; and with this goes no more dialogue than is needed—a bare line or two might at a pinch be omitted—for illustration. Cominius in six lines—

> Breathe you, my friends: well fought; we are come off
> Like Romans, neither foolish in our stands,
> Nor cowardly in retire: believe me, sirs,
> We shall be charged again. Whiles we have struck,
> By interims and conveying gusts we have heard
> The charges of our friends.

—is made to tell us what we need to know of his share in the battle and its further prospects, to paint us himself as general (just such a one as Marcius is not; the contrast striking), to tell us something besides of the lie of the battlefield, even of the weather! When Corioles has been taken, and Marcius is speeding Cominius' aid and the discomfiture of Aufidius, old Titus Lartius, with him his general's drummer and trumpeter, a scout also, distinguished by his light running gear, come from the inner to the outer stage, an officer and some more soldiers following:

> So, let the ports be guarded: keep your duties
> As I have set them down. If I do send, dispatch
> Those centuries to our aid; the rest will serve

> For a short holding; if we lose the field,
> We cannot keep the town. . . .
> Hence, and shut your gates upon us.
> Our guider, come; to the Roman camp conduct us.

Seven lines of speech, together with the significance of the figures and their movement—away from the city: back into it; the closing of the gates—suffice for this taste of Roman caution and cool judgment in warfare. The contrast is to come this time in the next scene's furious duel between Marcius and Aufidius.

The verse in general is meaty and lean; it contains few images and is all but free of extended metaphor. Its quality of direct attack is a strength to the actor. As an instance:

> Officious, and not valiant; you have shamed me
> In your condemned seconds.

—for Aufidius, left standing there while Marcius triumphantly pursues the unwelcome interlopers, the least wordiness would seem weakness; but that one spare sentence an actor can pack with spleen.

Marcius' magnanimity is given as direct and simple expression. The battle over:

> I sometime lay here in Corioles
> At a poor man's house; he used me kindly.
> He cried to me; I saw him prisoner.
> But then Aufidius was within my view,
> And wrath o'erwhelmed my pity. I request you
> To give my poor host freedom.

It makes part—with the immediate weary-minded forgetting of the man's name; has he not the right to be weary!—of the upbuilding of his character, is a counterpart to that scornful rating of the commoners. And the

verse accommodates this; as it does his joking response
to the army's acclaim of him:

> I will go wash;
> And when my face is fair you shall perceive
> Whether I blush or no.

as it will later his lovingly ironic reproof to his wife's
tears of welcome:

> Wouldst thou have laughed had I come coffin'd home,
> That weeps't to see me triumph? ...

Surely the very perfection of such simplicity!

The play contains little or no superfluous matter. With
the civic struggle at full pitch, the effect to be made one
of riot and confusion, each character, either chorus of
Senators and plebeians, contributes exactly to the scene's
need.

> BRUTUS.   Aediles, seize him!
> CITIZENS.   Yield, Marcius, yield!
> MENENIUS.   Hear me one word;
>   Beseech you, Tribunes, hear me but one word.
> AEDILES.   Peace, peace!
> MENENIUS. Be that you seem, truly your country's friend,
>   And temperately proceed to what you would
>   Thus violently redress.
> BRUTUS.   Sir, these cold ways,
>   That seem like prudent helps, are very poisonous
>   Where the disease is violent. Lay hands upon him,
>   And bear him to the rock.
> MARCIUS.   No, I'll die here.
>   There's some among you have beheld me fighting:
>   Come, try upon yourselves what you have seen me.
> MENENIUS. Down with that sword! Tribunes, withdraw
>   awhile.

BRUTUS.   Lay hands upon him.
MENENIUS.   Help Marcius! Help!
You that be noble, help him, young and old!
CITIZENS. Down with him! Down with him!

In this mutiny, the Tribunes, the Aediles, and the People are beat in.

The passage is scored as it might be for an orchestra, each instrument given its task: Brutus' sharp order, reinforced by the plebeians' shout; Menenius' half-heard remonstrance; the Aediles' command for the silence in which Menenius and Brutus exchange their acid arguments; this sharply broken again by Brutus. And no shout follows now; since Marcius, mute and motionless so far, suddenly draws his sword and challenges combat. Circumspect old Menenius presses peace on both parties. It is Brutus who is reckless and hounds on his outnumbering mob. Then, for Menenius, if it is to come to fighting, each must stand to his own side. And the fit few prove too much for the many.

THE DYNAMIC PHRASE

Spare dialogue need not be poor dialogue. The little said can be made to suggest much left unsaid. Dramatic art matures to this. In the cruder sort of play the characters will often not be fully dramatized, the dramatist himself to be heard speaking through them too plainly. But when they are, and their speech is authentically their own, then, by planning and a close collaboration with the actor, it can be brought to the expression of the implicit too, of those confusions of thought that trouble men, of feelings that never, in life, find words. The expression must be kept seemingly lifelike, not translated into overexplicit—into explanatory—terms: this would falsify the effect of it. The art of the dramatist lies in the discovering of more covert means.

The dynamic phrase, into which the actor is to pack the effect of a cumulated mass of thought and feeling, is one means. Shakespeare early learned the use of it. When Romeo hears of Juliet's death:

> Is it even so? Then I defy you, stars!

rhetoric will follow later; but nothing of such deep and suggestive feeling. Falstaff's

> Master Shallow, I owe you a thousand pound.

is a line of the sort, with its comically generous divining of Master Shallow's feelings too. So, when he has watched Cressid dallying with Diomed, is Troilus' response to Ulysses' 'All's done, my lord', his grim 'It is.'

The dynamic phrase can be used in more ways than one. And there is purer tragedy in Macduff's cold

> He has no children.

than in all his throbbing grief for his loss of them. Macbeth's own response to what once his servants would hardly have dared tell him:

> The Queen, my lord, is dead.

is no more than a silence, to be followed—when that bitter emptiness, his loss of the very power to feel, has made itself felt—by the wearily impatient

> She should have died hereafter;
> There would have been a time for such a word. . . .

and some detached reflections upon the meaninglessness of life. The effect—as of spiritual impotence—is not simply in these. To gain it, the underlying tragedy has been the play's length in development.

In a play, text apart from context may lose most of its meaning. The story itself, with Shakespeare, will run directly and openly along; there is no plot (the term will be misleading) to be spun and unravelled.[63] The play's structure is built up by the interlocking of character and event, and the opposition of character to character; this gives it body, balance and strength. In *Coriolanus* the main stresses are between Marcius and the Senate on the one side, the people on the other; this beside, between Marcius and Aufidius, Marcius and Volumnia, jolly Menenius and the sour Tribunes. These are plain to be seen, and they implement the action. But there is much of auxiliary consequence as well, not set out at length or very explicitly, left latent, rather, for the actors to develop or elucidate in their acting.

The dramatist plans the essentials of this auxiliary action. Directions for it will be implicit in those passages of thrifty dialogue and their context; but only as realized and expanded will its full significance be made clear. When, for instance, in the play's first scene Marcius and Cominius and the Senators come together, their conduct to each other, the friendly yielding of precedence, Marcius' show of respect for the Consul and 'our best elders', his easy acceptance otherwise of his own heroic eminence, and (pointed omission telling too) the ignoring of the new Tribunes—twenty pregnant lines and their acting suffice to picture us men and party; and not even the anonymous among them are left lay figures.

So it is with the triumphal entry after the victory at Corioles. Action and speech are knit together, the one clarifying and enhancing the other. The shouts of welcome hushed, Marcius' look is turned—ours too again—to the women modestly withdrawn there; Roman mother and wife, the harsh Volumnia shaken by emotion, Virgilia happily weeping. Then he, Rome's hero, kneels dutifully to his mother, dries his wife's tears with words of gentle, magnanimously grave irony, frees himself from that mood with a joke for Menenius, his courteous bow to Valeria. More telling too will be this second ignoring of the Tribunes (on a third occasion, Marcius, confident of his consulship, will openly voice his contempt for them). Again, it is a matter of thirty-five lines or less. Yet not only their own significance, their illustration and the interplay of the response they demand, brings every participant in the scene into helping to give it life.

Shakespeare has come to demanding more of his actors, and to giving them more—though it may be less ostensible—opportunity. He demands their imaginative collaboration, leaves much to their discretion, gives them outlines to colour in lightly or heavily. How large a part, for instance, does wine-flushed stubbornness play in Aufidius' repeated refusal to recognize the unmuffled Marcius, waiting by his hearth in Antium? The actor may decide. The text leaves him latitude and discretion, Shakespeare providing neither comment nor response to clinch the matter.

When Menenius returns with Volumnia and Virgilia from parting with the banished Marcius at the city gate: the strain now relaxed, the day lost, old age in him suddenly gives way; and against their vituperatings he can only set a 'Peace, peace! be not so loud', a 'Come, come; peace!'; and finally, the triumphant Tribunes departing, a

> You have told them home;
> And, by my troth, you have cause. You'll sup with me?

With no more to be done, there's left at least the comfort of a meal! The mere words given their surface meaning do little more than somewhat superfluously help the action on. But as bits of material to be used for filling out the figure of Menenius a skilful actor can put them to lively use. And that final consolatory bidding to supper then becomes also the better springboard for the grim, indomitable

> Anger's my meat; I sup upon myself,
> And so shall starve with feeding.

by which—its immediate effect besides—we shall be helped to keep Volumnia vividly in mind during her coming absence from the action.

The actor thus potently collaborating, one scene can be made to feed others that follow, and repeated expounding be avoided. Aufidius' backsliding from Marcius as they march together upon Rome is fully set out in his talk with his Lieutenant. After this merely his watchful presence through successive scenes will be eloquent, and the few cold phrases with which he breaks its silence need no enlarging: for example, his dry approbation of Marcius' rebuffing of Menenius with that

> You keep a constant temper.

his ironic sympathy for the son's breaking at last under the mother's pleading:

> I was moved withal.

A moment later comes an aside as explicit as was the talk with the Lieutenant:

> I am glad thou hast set thy mercy and thy honour
> At difference in thee: out of that I'll work
> Myself a former fortune.

and this keeps the trend of the action incontestably clear. But his open share in the two scenes, those two dry sentences (and one other) which positively do little more than emphasize his continuing presence, these an

Aufidius can discreetly colour, can most effectively
charge with the strange blend of hatred and admiration
that we know possesses the man. Such acting it is that
adds something of another dimension to the personified
narrative of a play, a dimension of being.

A speech may have an auxiliary sense, to which the
actor must give value by his own particular means.
When Marcius has finally yielded Rome's fate to Volumnia's plea he knows—and we are aware—that he has
also put his own in Aufidius' hands. He turns to him:

> Aufidius, though I cannot make true wars,
> I'll frame convenient peace. Now, good Aufidius,
> Were you in my stead, would you have heard
> A mother less, or granted less, Aufidius?

The expressed resolve beside, in the mere repetitions of
that 'Aufidius', as the actor can give them varying
cadence, will sound all the pleading on his own behalf—
it is little!—that Marcius' pride could ever let him make.

To hark back to his banishment: much of the preceding scene is but preparation for the promised self-control
of the curt

> I am content.

with which on his return to the market place he answers
the Tribunes' provocative demand:

> If you submit you to the people's voices,
> Allow their officers, and are content
> To suffer lawful censure for such faults
> As shall be proved upon you?

for the countering too, a little later, of a yet more
insolently peremptory

> Answer to us.

with the measured

> Say then; 'tis true. I ought so.

Such effects of self-control can, it is obvious, only be convincingly made when the elements of something to control have already been as convincingly built into the character.

THE USE OF SILENCE

Shakespeare has learned to put silence to a variety of uses. Although, later in this same scene, intolerably stung by that 'traitor to the people', Marcius finally forswears his promised temperance, yet he stands rigidly silent while Sicinius

> in the name o' the people,
> And in the power of us the Tribunes ...

passes formal sentence of banishment upon him, while the people ratify it with a chorused

> It shall be so.

Thus he multiplies many times—when anger finally does break bounds—the effect of his

> You common cry of curs! whose breath I hate ...

And there is the silence to which the unhappy Tribunes are reduced when, while Cominius and Menenius mock them, the news accumulates that this once-banished Marcius is marching with the Volscians upon Rome— one meek

> But is this true, sir?

from Brutus, put in to emphasize it. There is most particularly the

Holds her by the hand, silent.

—Shakespeare's own direction, that rarity! It is no more than a simple gesture, with which Marcius accepts the doom his surrender to his mother brings on him; a mere silence, yet it is the culminating moment of the play.

In the vivifying of such silences, the imaginative use of the 'dynamic phrase' with its pent emotions, expressing things left latent, in the general demand now made upon the actor that he altogether assimilate himself to the character he is presenting, much is changed from the earlier illustrative declaiming of verse or prose. Yet Shakespeare's is, and remains through all changes, the drama of eloquence. And his art's chief achievement in this kind has been to turn eloquence for its own sake into a *relative* eloquence (so to call it) springing, seemingly spontaneously, from character-enlivening occasion; the poetic form not broken, set free rather to be as personal and malleable a medium of expression as may be.

DRAMATICALLY LEGITIMATE ELOQUENCE

The story of *Coriolanus* is pre-eminently one of public life; and throughout the play—from Menenius' persuasive tale of the Belly and the Members to Marcius' last desperate haranguing of his Volscian masters—scene after scene offers dramatically legitimate occasion for eloquence. There is much variety of occasion too, as of speaker and temper of speech; the mutiny of the citizens, so differently dealt with by Menenius and Marcius; the crisis on the battlefield, the thanks to Marcius for his great part in the victory, later the public address to him with its carefully sought phrases; the war of words between Marcius and the Tribunes; Volumnia's spitfire retorting on them, to find contrast later in her stern, measured defence of Rome; Marcius finally brought to bay, fatally unchanged—here are many sorts of eloquence validly provided for. But there will be—and as legitimately—more likeness than difference in the matter of it, and between the speakers. For Menenius, Cominius and the Tribunes, Marcius and his mother, even the Volscians and Aufidius look—if not always from one standpoint—all towards the same horizon. There is the difference, truly, that less bitterness goes to battling against Volscian neighbours without the gates than against enemy kindred within. And this likeness lends to the temper of the verse a consistency which Marcius' own inevitable domination of it will but confirm, since there is little to be expressed in him that outranges the scope of the rest. And here again the close-woven pattern of event and character, the internecine in the struggle, is an element of the tragedy.

There is nothing profound in Marcius, nor anything to set him inwardly apart from friend or foe, and all introspection is foreign to him. Of his two brief soliloquies, one is little more than an outburst of febrile ill-temper, a climax to his infatuate protest against donning the gown of humility and asking the citizens for their votes:

> Better it is to die, better to starve,
> Than crave the hire which first we do deserve.
> Why in this woolvish gown should I stand here,
> To beg of Hob and Dick, that does appear,
> Their needless vouches? . . .

—and the exceptional succession of six rhymed couplets with their jangling iteration goes to painting this. The second is detached comment, hardly more. He is in Antium, the revolution within him already accomplished.

> O world, thy slippery turns! . . .

If we hear of no doubts or misgivings or struggles of conscience it is because there will have been none. Plunged in misery,

> Longer to live most weary . . .

by a sudden 'slippery turn' he has become—so he supposes—another man:

> My birth-place hate I, and my love's upon
> This enemy town.

It is as simple as that. Of the workings of a troubled mind he knows no more than does a child. He is frank and direct with mother, wife or friend, eloquent in anger. Of the inward Marcius we have passing glimpses only; in his thought for his one-time host in Corioles, for the widows his valour has left grieving there; in his respect for his mother, his chaste love for his wife; finally in the resigned realization of

> Not of a woman's tenderness to be,
> Requires nor child nor woman's face to see.

—its reflective cadence throwing it gently into relief against the stronger rhythm of the current speech.

The Question of Act-Division

THE play's action falls dramatically into three main divisions. The first, after some preliminary excursions into the citizens' discontent, covers the Volscian war; the second begins with Marcius' triumphant return from it, develops the struggle around his consulship and finishes upon his banishment; the third runs from his surrender to Aufidius, through the threats and alarms of his return, the surrender to his mother and the catastrophe of the end. This, however, being among the plays first found in the Folio, is there submitted to the formal five-act division—which, lacking more than once any dramatic warrant, one doubts to be Shakespeare's. A tricky question to answer, this of act-division; since we do not very certainly know how, at performances—and with what consistency—the act-pause was used. As a ten-minute interval during which the audience could relax? As a more formal minute's breathing-space for the actors? The punctuating power of the act-division will differ greatly.

What dramatic value can there be in the Folio's division here that parts Act II from Act III? In the action itself there is continuity. In Marcius' own tones and in his friends' attitude towards him, their deference to him as 'Lord Consul', his readiness for more war with the Volscians, one may perhaps distinguish a change of key; but nothing, one would say that needs an act-division— certainly not a long pause—for its emphasis. Again, a fresh dramatic chapter in the story certainly begins with Coriolanus' appearance at Antium, *in mean apparel, disguised and muffled.* Just before this comes the 'bridge scene' between the Roman and Volscian spies; and, from a dramatic standpoint, the Folio could suitably either end its third act with this or begin its fourth. It does neither. And if the practical convenience of a Marcius who must doff his Consul's insignia to make himself all but unrecognizable in his mean apparel ought also to be considered—it is not. Nor does there seem to be any very patent dramatic reason for ending a fourth act where the Folio ends this, nor for beginning the fifth act with Menenius setting forth on his errand after refusing to.

We may feel certain, surely, that Shakespeare sought, first and last, to make his plays dramatically viable, although we may not be so certain as we begin to think we are of the effects made by his stage on his stagecraft. But when we can be fairly certain of this, it is good evidence that what offends against these effects is not from his hand.

The Stage Directions

SOME of these are among the play's most notable features. Incidentally, their dramatic value apart, they stand among the items of evidence of a retirement to Stratford and the writing of the latest plays in a semi-detachment from the theatre. Such evidence is, of course, inferential, no better than guesswork if you will. But *Coriolanus* at least speaks in this respect pretty plainly of a manuscript to be sent to London, and of a staging which the author did not expect to supervise himself.

The directions are always expert, devised by someone who has visualized the action very clearly. They may be such a mere memorandum as a prompter might write in, as where, in the passage covering the battle for Corioles, after the customary indicative

> *The fight is renewed. The Volsces retire into Corioles, and Marcius follows them to the gates.*

comes for Marcius the mandatory

> *Enter the gates.*

One builds nothing on that. But

> *Enter Cominius, as it were in retire, with soldiers.*

and later

> *Enter two Officers, to lay cushions, as it were, in the Capitol.*

—these 'as it weres' are, so to say, 'advisory'; the actors must devise their expression for themselves. On the other hand, action of dramatic importance may be underlined, though the spoken text indicate it clearly enough:

> *Enter Coriolanus, in a gown of humility . . .*

and the next words spoken are

> Here he comes, and in the gown of humility. . . .

And later—though nothing will be plainer than the sight itself—

> *Enter Coriolanus, in mean apparel, disguised and muffled.*

Here is the author, stressing these effects upon the actors, for his own satisfaction, to make sure they miss none of them; for his own great satisfaction, one feels, when it comes to

> *Draw both the Conspirators and kils Martius, who falles, Auffidius stands on him.*

And

> *Enter Menenius to the Watch or Guard.*

'*Watch or Guard*'; whichever you please, it comes to the same thing.

But the direction to be valued most of all is that given to the actor of Marcius himself. Before he yields to Volumnia he

> *Holds her by the hand, silent.*

—for an appreciable moment, it must be. Had Shakespeare had his actors at hand to direct should we now ever have had that? Did a foolishly rash Macbeth go speeding on after the sledge-hammer blow of

> The Queen, my lord, is dead.

Not if Shakespeare was there to stop him!

Corry-ols, Corry-o-les, or Corī-o-les; Corry-o-lanus or Corī-o-lanus?

IT is related of John Philip Kemble that once, when making at the end of a performance the customary announcement of the next, he told the house that the company would present Shakespeare's play of Corry-o-lanus in which we himself would undertake the part of Corī-o-lanus.[64] Such disputes would occasionally enliven the already livelier theatre of those days, resembling as it could—the 'Pit' of it—rather an unruly club than a mere shop in which plays are so tamely bought and sold. And while, despite three centuries of searching out—and wilfully creating!—Shakespearean problems, there remain more than enough to be solved, few, whether of greater or less import, offer us such a free choice as does this. Nor is it of such little dramatic import as the pronunciation of a word will commonly be. It proclaims the hero's glory; its refusal to him is the final insult which he will not brook; at a dozen moments it is made the keynote of eloquence and emotion. The cadence of the word, and its music; those, therefore, are, dramatically, the two important things about it. Whatever Shakespeare's intention, we may be certain that he meant it to sound well.

It is not first met with precisely in that form, but coming from a Volscian Senator in his jaunty

Let us alone to guard Cor-ī-oles. . . .

which is as simple a decasyllable as the play contains. But when, two scenes later, a messenger enters with his news, this is that

> The citizens of Corry-ols have issued,
> And given to Lartius and to Marcius battle....

and the minor actor who did anything but stress the 'Corry...' might count, surely, upon sharp correction. Yet only twenty-three lines later Marcius will be all but bound to say that Titus Lartius is

> Holding Co-ri-o-les in the name of Rome...

—and would possibly not be so amenable to correction. And a little later he tells Aufidius,

> Within these three hours, Tullus,
> Alone I fought in your Co-ri-o-les walls....

And what other than the longest of long i's can that Corioles contain?

But here, of course, are sources only of the 'Coriolanus' of our question; and this, when it first appears a scene later, still is so much a proclamation (with an exulting echo) that it can be counted out of the verse and its demands altogether. One can only say that as it is surrounded by 'Corioles' (one before and two after), with their long i's indubitable, 'Coriolanus' would seem to be the most instinctive derivative.

It comes again in the verse of a proclamation; and the Herald may have it either way he will—or both.

> Know, Rome, that all alone Marcius did fight
> Within Corioles gates, where he hath won...

(there is the long ī undoubtedly)

> With fame, a name to Caius Marcius: these
> In honour follows Corry-o-lanus.

with, to conclude, either a

> Welcome to Rome, renownèd Corry-o-lanus!

or a

> Welcome to Rome, renowned Cor-ī-olanus!

which you choose; Volumnia also having her choice
between a poor line in

> What is it? Corry-o-lanus must I call thee?

and a better one in

> What is't? Cor-ī-olanus must I call thee?

—being sure, in rehearsal at any rate, of loud ironic
protests from the rest of the company when, with a wink,
she poses the problem!

Thereafter, however, and on all hands, the pronunciation 'Corry-o-lanus' slides more easily into the verse,
though never stimulating it. Sicinius can even squeeze a
certain mockery into the tunelessness of

> Your Corry-olanus is not much missed
> But with his friends. . . .

Again, Volumnia will do the better with

> To his surname Cor-ī-olanus longs more pride
> Than pity to our prayers.

though the verse does not force it on her, and fits the
word ill at best. But 'Cor-ī-o-les', a minute later, it must
be.

With the play's closing moments we are nearing the
name's most pointedly dramatic use. Aufidius'

> Ay, Marcius, Caius Marcius. Dost thou think
> I'll grace thee with that robbery, thy stolen name
> Coriolanus in Corioles?

'Corry-o-lanus in Corry-ols' or 'Corry-o-les' it certainly
cannot be; 'Corry-o-lanus in Cor-i-o-les' it just may be.

But how much finer 'Cor-ī-olanus in Cor-ī-o-les'! And
what Marcius will hesitate an instant over

> 'Boy'! false hound!
> If you have writ your annals true, 'tis there,
> That, like an eagle in a dove-cote, I
> Fluttered your Volscians in Cor-ī-o-les. . . .

'Corry-o-lanus', then, it would seem has the majority of
voices. But let there never be one for 'Corry-ols' or
'Corry-o-les'!

One is tempted towards what is, doubtless, an indefen-
sible heresy. Were the Elizabethans as inconsistent in the
pronouncing of some uncommon words as in the spelling
of them? Was it as possible for an actor to say 'Corry-o-
lanus' at one moment and 'Cor-ī-olanus' at another—
whichever suited the verse the better—with none of the
hearers finding the change objectionable as it would be for
a dramatist to sign himself 'Shakespeare' at one moment
and 'Shaxpeer' the next? It would need, of course, a braver
man than the present writer to plead this.

Notes

1 And even Henry V, at war, is not seen fighting. He is the
   didactic hero, and this is far less mature dramatic work.
2 And it is pretty certainly Shakespeare's own. Such moments
   of eloquent silence are to be found indicated, more or less
   explicitly, in all the later plays. A very notable one comes
   with Macbeth's hearing of his wife's death. Another follows
   upon the blow that Othello publicly deals Desdemona.
3 In *Cymbeline*, certainly, costume marks the difference between
   Roman and British, and in *Macbeth* between Scots and English; in *Antony and Cleopatra*, probably, between Roman and
   Egyptian. We may take for granted, I think, that Volscians
   and Romans were dressed distinctively. A 'realistic' reading
   may suggest that Marcius would cast off his Roman garb with

his allegiance. But I believe that, quitting the 'mean apparel' in which he went to encounter Aufidius, he would reappear as a Roman general, the dramatic effect being worth more than any logic.

4 It was not, truly, this division of the army which fled and left him to his fate 'within Corioles gates'. But while we shall remark the contrast in spirit and conduct, we shall not, I think—and are not meant to—make the nicer distinction.

5 Note, too, that there is something of the duellists' conventional salute in this, as it might be a clashing of sword against shield.

6 Tennyson finds a similar thought for

> His honour rooted in dishonour stood
> And faith, unfaithful, kept him falsely true.

7 What exactly is the effect that Shakespeare means to have made here? The mere suggestion of his danger in Marcius'

> O, mother, mother!
> What have you done? . . .

Volumnia, not yet certain of her victory, might easily overlook. But the repeated

> O, my mother, mother! O!
> You have won a happy victory to Rome;
> But for your son, believe it, O, believe it,
> Most dangerously you have with him prevailed,
> If not most mortal to him.

—to ignore this practically plain statement that he is most likely to be going to his death she must be prostrated indeed. And that I think on the whole is the intention. He then turns and goes to Aufidius, and Volumnia, left among the women, quickly recovers. She has not fainted, there must be no such weakness; it is simply a moment's reaction from the extreme strain of the victory. He turns back, and apostrophizes them from where he stands:

> O, mother! wife!

and stands still gazing while Aufidius speaks his aside. This is the heartfelt farewell he takes.

Editors hereabouts insert

The Ladies make signs to Coriolanus.

presumably to account for the 'Ay, by and by . . . ' with which he breaks the silence of his gaze. They stand expectantly where he has left them; there is no need of more. Then he joins them, as if bidding them dismiss all forebodings, gallantly congratulating them on their victory; and our query, if there was risk of one: why does not Volumnia see that in saving Rome she has sent her son to his death? has been fended off. It may return on reflection when the play is over. It probably will not. And if it takes the shape of the memory of a Volumnia as peremptory and passionate as her son, as stubborn in her own cause and as oblivious to all besides, that is a not unjust one.

Shakespeare the practical playwright, having had his full use of a character, and the whole action being near its end, will add nothing needlessly. Volumnia has saved Rome, and the action asks no more of her. Care for her son's fate would prolong or complicate it, and, in doing so, upset the balance of interest. It must suffice, then, that we do not remark any such omission; and circumstance and character are shaped so that we shall not. It is in these instances of dramatic tact that Shakespeare the playwright shows at his most skilful.

8 Later on, in Antium, Aufidius makes it 'Twelve several times' that he has been beaten. But nothing hangs on the precise number, and he is not on his oath.

9 One or two lines in this last speech are doubtless corrupt. But rectify them as we may, we shall hardly make them lucid.

10 Shakespeare's own stage direction, we may once more be pretty sure.

11 For the argument that those and other stage directions are Shakespeare's own, see p. 202ff.

12 For the implicit contrast with the scene between Charmian, Iras, Alexas and the Soothsayer in *Antony and Cleopatra*, see pp. 31-2.

13 The ordering of the action upon Shakespeare's stage must be gathered by piecing together text, stage directions and our

yet imperfect and disputed knowledge of the mechanics of the Globe.

The stage directions are for the most part figurative and recommendatory, not set down by the book-holder or in his fashion (see p. 202ff.). The curtains to the inner stage could no doubt be made to serve, but it looks as if this Corioles had solid gates.

Enter the army of the Volsces.

might, by convention, mean that these opened to discover the dozen men or less who made the army standing there; and this, for the short time the text allows, would be convenient. It fits, too, the First Senator's

our gates,
Which yet seem shut, we have but pinn'd with rushes;
They'll open of themselves.

They could—wide enough to let the men through, and close behind them. This looks likely, and that they reopen later to accommodate the retreat—

*The Volsces retire into Corioles and Marcius follows
them to the gates.*

—and then stay open, to suit Marcius'

So, *now* the gates are ope: now prove good seconds:
'Tis for the followers fortune widens them,
Not for the fliers. . . .

until they shut on him.

The Romans are beat back to their trenches apparently through one of the side doors, the Volsces following them. It would need to be of some width to allow for the mêlée of men, swords and shields, and they might more conveniently be fought to a standstill on the stage. But *Enter Marcius, cursing*, contradicts this possibility. He has been beaten off too, the last of the Romans to go. Further, Titus Lartius is absent when he is shut in the city.

A textual note. In the line

> we'll beat them to their wives,
> As they us to our trenches follows.

(some editors preferring 'follow', others 'followed'). The 'follows' has probably slipped in by some accident from the neighbouring stage direction, *Marcius follows them to the gates*. Neither sense nor verse accommodates its speaking.

14 The *exeunt* occasionally marked for the spoilers after 'I took this for silver' is an editorial interpolation and not in the Folio.

15 How, in the terms of Shakespeare's theatre, is this vacating of the stage, which marks the end of a scene and change of place, differentiated from that of a few lines earlier, before the entry of the soldiers with their spoils, which indicated neither? In the first instance, probably, the open gates still confront us; in the second, after Titus Lartius and his attendants have passed through them, not only will they be closed, but the curtain masking the inner stage will be drawn too.

16 Time, as usual with Shakespeare in such cases, is elastic. We are to picture the Messenger and Marcius dashing across country; so they are allowed likely time for this. As to Titus Lartius' work of making good the city, issuing decrees and the rest of it, that, like the unquestioned minutes of a meeting, we 'take as read'.

17 There is corruption to the text hereabouts. When the soldiers take him up in their arms:

> Oh, me alone, make you a sword of me?

has found (to my mind) no very satisfactory interpretation or amendment.

> If these shows be not outward . . .

marks the touch of doubt; and there may be some connection of thought between this and the corrupt line.

Another corruption must be in the line

> Please you to march;
> And four shall quickly draw out my command. . . .

Why 'four'? The 'Please you to march' is worth noting too, with its unusual suavity.

18 Once more Shakespeare, by an incidental stroke, regulates
the clock of the action.

> Within these three hours, Tullus,
> Alone I fought in your Corioles walls. . . .

The echo from *Troilus and Cressida* is in

> Wert thou the Hector
> That was the whip of your bragged progeny. . . .

It may even perhaps echo Hector's own

> You wisest Grecians, pardon me this brag. . . .

19 So, but for amended spelling, the Folio. Capell, it seems,
added . . . *and other Romans*, and some editors have copied him.
But Shakespeare evidently wishes—be it by an arbitrary effect
only—to contrast Cominius and his officers and men, with
the solitary figure of Marcius, once more wounded.

The stage directions hereabouts tend to be emblematic.
How precise a meaning Shakespeare's audience would read
into *Flourishes and Alarums. A Retreat is sounded*, and the like, it
is hard for us to estimate. A few lines later, moreover, we
have *Enter Titus with his Power from the Pursuit*. Could there
have been any means of illustrating . . . *from the Pursuit*? I fancy
this is simple narrative.

20 It is likelier that *A flourish. Cornets.* rightly belongs to the end
of the scene before rather than to the beginning of this, which
certainly seems not to call for any sort of 'flourish'.

21 Shakespeare has been by no means sparing of space in this
scene so far. In particular he could have lessened the passage
between Menenius and the Tribunes by half and kept all its
substance. Is there any reason for this? He may, one suspects,
have been sure of an exceptionally good actor for Menenius.
Throughout the play he indulges the character and spacious-
ly—in incidental opportunities. Unfounded surmise, no more;
but it is somewhat as if he felt he safely could. Another and
more technical reason here, if any at all be needed, is at least
worth canvassing. We have left Marcius bloody and unkempt
after his fighting. The actor must have time to put himself in

proper array for his triumphal entry. Will the speaking of 190 lines allow him more than enough? And here the question of act-division—between I and II—is also involved. Is this Shakespeare's, or an editor's? And if Shakespeare's, and to be marked in performance, was an appreciable interval allowed or no? Speculative questions, and of no capital importance; pertaining to the play's study, nevertheless. For the main question of act-division, see p.200ff.

22 *Titus Lartius?* A slip, apparently, on Shakespeare's part. Menenius tells us later that he has been sent for, and, a scene later still, he arrives, to be questioned by Coriolanus about Tullus Aufidius and the Volscian preparation for revenge.

23 There is an inconsistency in the stage directions here to be noted. The Folio marks an *Enter Brutus and Sicinius*, having accorded them no certain *exeunt*. Nothing very out of the way in this; both Folio and Quartos abound in such apparent slips. But it opens up a question of the movements and the placing of the two during the interchange between Menenius and Volumnia, and next while Marcius dominates the scene. They are still there, of course, when Menenius addresses them with his

> God save your good worships! Marcius is coming home.

But are they when he cites them to Marcius for the

> old crab-trees here at home that will not
> Be grafted to your relish....

If not, but for a responsive shrug or the like, Marcius' neglect of them will be purely negative. It looks, however, as if they were intended still, at this moment, to be thereabouts, glowering in the background. And probably they go off with the procession, hang back from it, and immediately return. This will at least justify the Folio's stage direction and give point to Brutus' sequent speech, his description of the hero's greeting by the crowd.

24 *To lay cushions, as it were*... is one among the play's 'suggestive' stage directions. A cushion can mean 'the seat of a judge or ruler' (though the reference for this definition in the O.E.D.

is dated 1659). Presumably the officers have a couple of actual cushions, or more, to lay. But the phrase has, I fancy, a further implication; it tells us—even as the subsequent dialogue shows—the sort of persons they are, not menials, but men of a definite dignity, the equivalent, possibly, in Shakespeare's mind, to officers of Parliament, who may bring to their covenanted respect for its members, Lords or Commons, a very critical private view of their individual worth.

25 At Cominius' command the procession moved 'on to the Capitol'. Brutus and Sicinius, after a fifty-five-line talk, are summoned there also, because

> 'Tis thought
> That Marcius shall be Consul.

and the thirty-five-line talk between the Officers lets them arrive in time for the business. Menenius' 'This our after-meeting . . .' implies that more has been happening, and associates the public thanks to Coriolanus and his proposal as Consul with the general business of the State, and lends them verisimilitude and importance thereby.

26 'Without a moment's heed . . .': this is sufficiently indicated in the continuity of the verse. Marcius' 'I do beseech you . . .' completing Menenius' line. Besides which (the actor will remember) Brutus has

> heard him swear,
> Were he to stand for Consul, never would he
> Appear i' the market place, nor on him put
> The napless vesture of humility . . .

27 But here Shakespeare performs one of his occasionally con-venient feats of sleight of hand. The Tribunes quit the stage with this intention; but immediately after the citizens enter, as in the market place, expecting Marcius, who shortly ar-rives. There has been no opportunity, then, for interference by the Tribunes—unless some break in the continuity of the action, some imaginary passage of time between the two scenes is to be conceded, and that can be counted out of the

question. Moreover, there is no sign in the talk of the citizens among themselves, or to Marcius, that Brutus and Sicinius have recently been at them. Yet, arriving later, when the ordeal is over and the 'voices' have been accorded, the two pointedly refer to the good advice they gave, and scold their already disillusioned followers for neglecting it.

> Could you not have told him
> As you were lessoned . . . ?
> Thus to have said,
> As you were fore-advised . . .

We probably do not detect the trick. But what brings Shakespeare to playing it? Is it that, having dispatched the Tribunes (so to say) to the market place, he sees how much better it may be to let the citizens encounter Marcius in his 'gown of humility' without their interference? Yet there is value in the present subsequent passage in which they expound and deplore the errors that, all against their advice, have been made, and undertake to relieve them. For it is in this that they give evidence of being 'masters o' the people' indeed. It will then become important not to prejudice its effect by staging shortly beforehand a similar passage of the actual giving of the good advice. Very well; that can be omitted, advantageously from other points of view also. And if it is also important to have the Tribunes reproach the citizens for ignoring their advice, let them do so. We are unlikely to remark later that the advice was never given, nor, as the action ran, could have been.

28 I doubt if any consistency of character can be established between the First or Second Citizens of the play's opening and of this scene, or between them in this and any of the later ones. Within the boundary of a single scene there will be consistency; they will be ineffectual figures otherwise. But to push the matter further would be to make each a character in his own right, so to speak, and to rob the populace of its collective strength. No matter how diverse the opinions and feelings to be vented, a crowd must remain dramatically a single if a multiple unit.

29 A point obscured in most modern editions by their setting the entrance of the citizens after the line has been spoken, whereas the Folio has them enter just before. It does not follow that he definitely intends them to hear it; he does not see them until immediately after. But they were there a moment before; he knows they are about. The point is that he does not care.

30 For the technical treatment of this soliloquy, see the section upon the play's verse, p. 179ff.

31 'Not for the first time': see p. 214, note 27.

32 If he is not at least willing for them to overhear, there is little or no point in the lines. But here is the schoolboy side of him, very similarly shown in the scene of the gown of humility.

33 There is significance in the two stage directions: first

> *Enter a rabble of Plebeians, with the Aediles.*

The people were assembled in the market place ready to disavow their choice of Coriolanus, but prepared—neither they nor the Tribunes—for no such business as this. So, called upon for help, they appear as a 'rabble'. It will be a very different matter when, for the later encounter, they have been 'collected . . . by tribes' and drilled in the required behaviour.

Secondly, while the plebeians are mustering to the support of their Tribunes, the direction to the Senators is

> *They all bustle about Coriolanus.*

It is one of the play's characteristically descriptive stage directions; and it suggests a certain embarrassment and fuss, the Senators little less perturbed than the Tribunes are.

34 Cominius, apparently, one. But I fancy that the

> Stand fast:
> We have as many friends as enemies.

is misascribed to him. For if not, he changes his mind barely a moment later; and, a little later still, a six-line speech conclusively puts him among the prudent ones. Further, he and Coriolanus depart together.

35 The Folio has marked an *exeunt* for Coriolanus and Cominius only; and the minor speeches immediately following are given to *Patri*, translated by later editors into First and Second Patrician, instead of to the Senators who have fulfilled this need till now. One queries at first an (unrecorded) departure of the Senators too; but at the end of the scene there still remains one Senator at least. A possible explanation is that the Senators in their robes—whatever on Shakespeare's stage these were—are meant to be withdrawn to the background, the gathering to lose the last of its ceremonial aspect. This will add, by contrast, to the semblance of authority worn by Brutus and Sicinius, reappearing at the head of their rabble.

36 The Folio's stage direction speaks here only of his entering *with Nobles*; actually it is later, on his way to banishment, that he is said to be accompanied to the city gate by *the young Nobility of Rome*. But the distinction implied at both points between them (whether called *Nobles* or *young Nobility*) and the rest of his party is the same, and its meaning is, I think, clear. At first he has, of course, the Senate on his side; and among the variously termed Patricians, Gentry, Nobles, some will be Senators, some not. Step by step, in his intransigence, he alienates the Senators, and—if it can be shown, if the theatre company can muster sufficient numbers—possibly some of the elders among the mere gentry too. But the young nobility— men more or less of his own age—side with him to the last. And it is at this point in the action that—though not much is made of it—they begin to be distinguished from the rest.

37 A simple effect, lost in the modern editorial delaying of her entrance by nine lines.

38 The exclamatory 'Better it is to die, better to starve ...' in the scene in the market place is hardly a soliloquy.

39 It is just possible, I think, that F's quaintly corrupted stage direction: *Exeunt Coriolanus, Cominius, with Cumaligs* (due to a muddled deletion in the MS evidently) has to do with the several other stage directions and hints in the text meant to indicate the growing division among Coriolanus' supporters (see above, note 36, and page 218, note 40). Was the *with* to have been followed by particulars of those that accompanied

him and those that did not, and did Shakespeare, for lack of room or any other likely reason, content himself rather with the *cum aliis*, leaving the fact that some went one way, some another to be deduced (and implemented by the actors) from the opening stage direction of the next scene: *Enter Coriolanus . . . with the young Nobility of Rome*; the elders, but for Cominius and Menenius, having definitely deserted him? Mere conjecture, and the point a small one; but the very smallest may have its worth in a reconstructing of the play's intended staging.

40 The young nobility, 'my friends of noble touch', here also left behind, are evidently closely related to the 'three or foure of his friends only' who, in North's Plutarch, did accompany him. The main point of the change is, of course, to bring Marcius, without more complication, to Antium all alone. A lesser dramatist might, then, have rid himself of the young nobility altogether. But to Shakespeare the enrichment of Marcius' character, slight as it is, by his dismissal of them at the gate, is worthwhile. And it costs him but half a line of text.

41 It is likely, I should say, that the sight of the young nobility returning from their farewell to Coriolanus at the city gate (to be followed in a minute by Volumnia, Virgilia and Menenius) and their demeanour when they see the Tribunes suggests this

> The nobility are vexed. . . .

to Sicinius. They would merely cross the stage. Cominius would presumably be with them. There is nothing, of course, either in text or stage direction to indicate this; but it fits with the rest of the scene's business. Clearly they should have appeared to follow Marcius to the gate, for he has said to them

> *when I am forth*,
> Bid me farewell, and smile.

42 The first and the last for that matter, even as the scene thus begun contains the play's sole soliloquy. A play of action, not reflection; by its nature it does not run to soliloquies.

One may note, in passing, the baldness of the introductory

> A goodly city is this Antium.

Shakespeare, in his maturity, is master of a dozen or more different ways of indirectly locating his scenes, as vaguely or as exactly as he may choose. But he will still use means as plain and direct as Sir Philip Sidney's notorious (and possibly apocryphal) placard, if they happen to be dramatically effective also.

43   At Antium lives he? . . .
      I would I had a cause to seek him there. . . .

—the unconsciously ironic words, spoken at the very height of his good fortune, may well have lodged in our minds.

Destitute, unarmed: Shakespeare does not stress the point of poverty, 'my misery' covering much more than that, if that; but the 'meanness' of his apparel, superfluous to mere disguise, seems meant loosely to suggest it. And it is evident that, in the encounter with Aufidius' servants, he at least wears no sword.

44 The phrase

            Some trick not worth an egg . . .

recalls Hamlet's

                      delicate and tender prince,
            Whose spirit with divine ambition puffed
            Makes mouths at the invisible event,
            Exposing what is mortal and unsure
            To all that fortune, death and danger dare,
            Even for an egg-shell . . .

It is not to say that there was, as he wrote, any constructive connection between the two in Shakespeare's mind, but the parallel is there; between Fortinbras the happy and Coriolanus the unhappy man of action, the one that (says Hamlet enviously) is ready

            greatly to find quarrel in a straw,
            When honour's at the stake . . .

his sense of honour exalting him, the other coming to see men and friends

            On a dissension of a doit, break out
            To bitterest enmity . . .

while his extravagant sense of his honourable duty to himself only betrays him to deep dishonour.

45 'Such flowery rhetoric': to Marcius, at any rate, in such a mood as he is, it will seem so. The contrast between the dry, angular phrasing of his speech to Aufidius and the rich, decorative and flowing melody of Aufidius' response is marked. A distinguished critic has connected—and somewhat carpingly—the dry angularity with the fact that Shakespeare took entire phrases for the speech from North's Plutarch, and used them unaltered. But this effect of a man speaking not spontaneously, as Aufidius does, but after long and bitter brooding with painful thought given to what he should say, speaking moreover not out of the fullness but the very emptiness of his heart, is, I suggest, precisely the effect meant to be made. And if Shakespeare found he could best make it by tacking together phrases from Plutarch he would certainly do so.

Marcius, at the thrilling moment of joining forces with Cominius on the battlefield before Corioles, had launched into something the same imagery that Aufidius uses now. But he was happily himself then as he will never be again. And, even so, that

> O, let me clip you
> In arms as sound as when I wooed, in heart
> As merry as when our nuptial day was done,
> And tapers turned to bedward.

denoted a harder temper than sounds from Aufidius'

> never man
> Sighed truer breath; but that I see thee here,
> Thou noble thing, more dances my rapt heart . . .

Shakespeare, in writing them, may or may not have had the likeness between the two passages in mind. It is unlikely that an audience will remark it.

46 Brutus and Sicinius are semi-comic characters, and the actors of them were, I think, expected to make their conspicuous silence here even more conspicuous by facial play.

47 Such now unusual phrases as 'not moving from the casque to the cushion' and 'even with the same austerity and garb as he controlled the war' increase for us the difficulty of following Aufidius' analysis of Coriolanus' virtues and defects, its repeated 'whether . . . s' making it already difficult enough. (The trick of the speech, one notes, is much that of Hamlet's 'So oft it chances in particular men. . . . ') And in quoting it here I have had, so as to isolate the continuity of thought, to reduce it to an ugly skeleton. Then, when it comes to the more general comments on success and failure, we meet with a corruption of the text—'hath not a tomb so evident as a chair . . . '—which no one yet, as far as I know, has been able satisfactorily to clarify. Altogether, it is a troublesome speech to the modern actor; and Aufidius, as a whole, may be called a troublesome character in the acting. Shakespeare, it seems, found him interesting, but would not afford space for his expansion (Cf. p. 57)

48 It is implied in more than one passage that the Tribunes now rule Rome, and Aufidius has just remarked of them that they 'are no soldiers'. Theirs is, in fact, what would be called today a 'pacifist' government, quite unprepared for war.

49 The Folio stage direction for the first scene is simply *Enter Coriolanus and Aufidius*. Capell added *and others*; and pretty plainly Coriolanus is not speaking to Aufidius alone. The council of war at a table set upon the inner stage is as easily deduced. The curtains will be closed as the two pass across the outer stage, finding Menenius there. They could be discovered when the curtains are drawn, the fifteen lines or so spoken by the Watch and Menenius allowing them that much time to take their places, or, having gone off by the side door, they can wait and enter again upon the inner stage.

50 The *in mourning habits* of the stage direction for this entrance is owed, apparently, to Capell. It implies veils, and is, I think, justified. The stage picture intended is not hard to reconstruct. Coriolanus will be seated at the council table on the inner stage surrounded by the contrastingly uniformed Volscian generals. The *Shout within* heralds the entry by a side door of the little group of veiled women and their attendants,

who stand facing him and more or less with their backs to the audience, so that the 'curtsy', and, upon Virgilia's unveiling, the 'doves' eyes' and Volumnia's 'bow' take effect more directly upon him than upon us. 'Describing them'; I do not, of course, mean to imply to the Volscian generals, but to himself and to us, as the convention of that stage allowed.

51 'Long as my exile . . . ,' he says later. Actually how long Shakespeare leaves indeterminate; but while the suggestion, when he comes to Aufidius in Antium, is that he has lost little time in doing so, here and hereabouts the implication is that, at any rate, much has changed in his absence. There is no need at either juncture to be exact, so that—open inconsistency avoided—the dramatic best can be made of each calendar.

52 This kneeling of each to other recalls Cordelia and King Lear. Shakespeare had found that in the old play about King Lear and his daughters. It clearly makes an affecting picture. Whether it was a favourite one with other dramatists of the time I am not well enough read to say. Whether or no, ceremonial kneeling was then in habitual use, and widely by comparison with the few occasions on which it is called for now.

53 To suggest this, by her mere appearance in the scene, with, for aid, the gemlike phrase describing her put into Coriolanus' mouth, seems to be her only use to it. But it is an incidental use of some little value; and since Shakespeare had her available, why not bring her on? One may even speculate whether the part itself does not chiefly owe its existence to such a fact as that the King's Men had, at this juncture, a boy in the company, who could both look and act it well. Even in these, their well-furnished days, they were unlikely to be overburdened with that sort of thing.

54 Note (once more) the visual effect of this, the contrast in the dress they wear, he the single Roman among these Volsces.

55 Were Shakespeare a didactic dramatist how well he might from this point build up his play to a moral and a happy ending: Marcius and his family reunited, Romans and Volsces clasping hands, peace over all! But he has the historic story

to deal with (Plutarch is not to be lightly treated) and the tragedy it involves—which, however, we must remark, is a tragedy, not wholly of character, but of character and circumstance combined.

Volumnia (of all people) urges reconciliation. Coriolanus is not the man to sponsor that; he can at best, he feels, stand aside and 'make convenient peace', But Aufidius also has to be reckoned with, and the Volscians who, for their part, want loot. It is in the fresh circumstances of the squabble over this that 'character' once more plays Coriolanus false, and Aufidius can seize the chance to kill him.

56 The Folio's stage directions leave him, by default, included in the general *Exeunt* a few lines later. But clearly he does not wait for Sicinius.

57 An earlier instance of this 'seeming spontaneity' in verse can be found in the Nurse in *Romeo and Juliet*. Really, it sometimes seems as if Shakespeare must have had all the secrets of his art stored in him from the beginning, as if he had only to enlarge upon what he already knew.

58 'Without *fundamental* loss': for some proof of this see Maeterlinck's translation of *Macbeth*. And Dover Wilson discovers in *As You Like It* the fossils of a verse version, of which Shakespeare presumably thought better.

59 'Convention and convenience': Blank verse may well, with a little practice, prove easier to write than formal prose; it is certainly easier to learn.

60 And here, it may be added, at the very opening of *Coriolanus*, is a 'set piece', in the story of the Belly and the Members. But it is put to direct dramatic use. The picture of Menenius cajoling the assembled citizens, to be contrasted immediately after with Marcius' swift hard way with them—the two passages together serve as a sort of opening statement of this aspect of the play.

61 It is evident, I think, that for the later plays Shakespeare had actors who could be relied upon to make good effect with these small but striking parts. There are several others in *Coriolanus*, some in *King Lear*, and a dozen or more in *Antony and Cleopatra*. They were doubled no doubt.

62 There is corruption in the text of the closing lines. But its elucidating would still leave the passage as a whole far from clear.

63 *Othello*, among the greater plays, really the single exception, nor fully an exception even so.

64 I have the story from that able, and now so deeply regretted, theatrical historian Harold Child.

Notes

Notes

Notes

Notes